The Mind Tree

The Mind Tree

A Miraculous Child Breaks the Silence of Autism

Tito Rajarshi Mukhopadhyay

Arcade Publishing • New York

For Dr Prathibha Karanth (Kaki) and Dr Veronica Mathias

FIRST NORTH AMERICAN EDITION 2003

Library of Congress Cataloging-in-Publication Data

Mukhopadhyay, Tito Rajarshi.
    The mind tree : a miraculous child breaks the silence of autism / Tito Rajarshi Mukhopadhyay. —1st North American ed.
        p. cm.
        ISBN 1-55970-699-6
        I. Autistic children—Literary collections. 2. Children's writings, American. I. Title.

    PS3613.U39M56 2003
    818'.603—dc21   2003052081

Published in the United States by Arcade Publishing, Inc., New York
Distributed by AOL Time Warner Book Group

Visit our Web site at www.arcadepub.com
Visit the author's Web site at www.canfoundation.org/tito

10 9 8 7 6 5 4 3 2 1

Designed by API

Text illustrations by John Fordham

EB

PRINTED IN THE UNITED STATES OF AMERICA

Contents

.

Editor's Note

To retain the integrity of Tito's writing, very little has been changed. Changes have only been made to ensure clarity, and brackets have been used where information has been added. *The Voice of Silence* was written when Tito was 8 years old, and *Beyond the Silence* when he was 11 years old. Tito turned 15 in July 2003.

A B C D E
F G H I J
K L M N O
P Q R S T U
V W X Y Z

Foreword

Rajarshi Mukhopadhyay, known as Tito, together with his mother, Soma, spent a day at Elliot House (The Centre for Social and Communication Disorders run by The National Autistic Society) in December 1999. The house was full that day. As well as the Elliot House staff, there was Dr Beate Hermelin, an expert in the field of autism and autistic savants, and a team from BBC television who were making a program about Tito.

Before Tito's visit, we had heard about him from Richard Mills, The National Autistic Society's Director of Services, who had met him and his family in India. We had also read some of his writings. We were intrigued, but inclined to be skeptical. There was no doubt that some individuals with autism have one or more remarkable talents far ahead of the rest of their abilities. However, these talents usually involve visuo-spatial or rote memory skills such as calendar calculations, numbers, drawing, remembering train timetables, and so on.

But Tito was apparently able to use long words in complex sentences and to express philosophical thoughts about life. This would not be too surprising in an adult with the pattern of behavior described by Asperger, with good expressive language and a high level of general ability. The remarkable point about Tito was that, at 11 years old, he could make only a few sounds that approximated to words. He had a few basic practical skills but was completely dependent on his parents, especially his mother. He had to be closely supervised and guided in social situations to make sure that his behavior was socially acceptable. His mother had taught him to read and write by using an alphabet board. From the age of six years he has written by himself using a pencil. [In addition to this book, he has written many others, often in verse, in his own handwriting.] He sometimes uses an alphabet board when interviewed, pointing to the letters while the words he spells are read out by his mother. The family speak both Bengali and English, and Tito spells his words in English.

When he arrived at Elliot House, Tito's observable behavior was exactly like that of a mute child with classic autism, ignoring people but exploring the objects that took his attention. Soma settled him down and wrote the alphabet on a piece of paper. We asked questions and Tito pointed to the letters to spell his replies. He did this independently, without any physical guidance from his mother. He replied to questions in full sentences, including long words used appropriately. He also spontaneously told us, in handwriting, that he wanted the book he had written to be published and demanded a promise that this would happen. Dr Judith Gould asked him to do the British Picture Vocabulary Scale, which requires the person doing the test to demonstrate the meaning of individual words or phrases by pointing to one of four possible pictures for each one. Tito reached the level achieved by people aged 19 years!

The contrast between Tito's overt, typically autistic behavior — at one point he grabbed my hand to use it as a mechanical tool to turn a stiff door handle — and the sophistication of the language expressed through his alphabet board was truly amazing. Soma had taught him intensively from the time he was about $2^{1}/_{2}$ years old. She used the technique, familiar to parents and teachers of children with autism, of moving his limbs through the motions needed for each task, including pointing, until he learnt the feel of the muscle movements. Tito himself has described his inability to initiate movements without such guidance. This seems to support the proponents of facilitated communication, who believe that all children with autistic disorders, however severely learning disabled they appear to be, are potentially capable of understanding and expressing complex ideas if helped by appropriate physical guidance.

It is important to emphasize that Tito showed, very early on, clear signs of good cognitive ability through his recognition of and ability to match numbers, letters and shapes. This encouraged his mother to work with him, using her truly remarkable intelligence, ingenuity and dedication, with the results we have seen. Children who do not exhibit any signs of good cognitive ability are very unlikely indeed to develop skills through any method of teaching, including facilitated communication. The fact that Tito began to write for himself at the age of six is corroboration of the fact that the ideas he expresses are his own.

Tito's writings are characteristic of someone with an autistic disorder in that they basically revolve around himself and his personal experiences. When one considers the physical and psychological disabilities he has to overcome, this self absorption is perhaps not so surprising. Despite this, his writing provides a vivid description of what it is like to be autistic and his thoughts about the meaning of life. It is essential reading for anyone wanting to understand the nature of autism.

Individuals with autistic disorders are endlessly fascinating. Those like Tito, with remarkable skills in contrast to their general level of disability, arouse feelings of wonder, astonishment and intellectual curiosity, which are among the many rewards experienced by those working in this field.

All of us who met Tito and Soma on that unforgettable day wish them both, for the future, every happiness and fulfillment of their ambitions.

Lorna Wing
Consultant Psychiatrist

The Voice of Silence

The Window of my World

Men and women are puzzled by everything I do. My parents and those who love me, are embarrassed and worried. Doctors use different terminologies to describe me. I just wonder.

The thoughts are bigger than my expressions to get a shape. Every move that I make interprets my helpless way to show how trapped I feel in the continuous flow of happenings. The happenings occur in a way that show the continuity of cause and effect. The effect of a cause becomes the cause of another effect. And I wonder. . . .

That is not just wonder alone but also a reason for my worry. I think about the little boy who had a way of expressing himself, not through speech but through a frustrated temper tantrum. The language was known but it did not relate to anything.

Shadows

The hand had made a strange relationship with its shadow, and he fluttered it and spent his hours, contented with the lone company of his shadow. And his worries stopped. He shut away the world and felt secure in the presence of the shadow. If only the world could be a game with the shadow! But the reality was that he was drawing himself away and away into the world of his shadow.

Nights were terrible. He searched everywhere for his shadow. He flapped to call it, there was nothing but darkness. He cried for it betrayed by the friend.

The next friend was the mother's lap, which had the warmth and readiness. It reached such a point that he was in a state of panic if somebody else tried to pick him up. He refused every place and also social gatherings. Even new roads, the garden and people were frightening. Mother forced him to socialise, by taking him to people's homes, and the situation got worse. The lap of mother should not be let off. The boy now refused to walk.

The effect of a small cause — but I realise a bad result of a good effort.

"My son spoke when he was five," somebody convinced his parents. "My neighbour's child spoke when he was three and half," said another voice. I specify 'voice' because he recognised voices rather than people. The relationship between voices and people developed later. That is an interesting story.

His mother used to sing and he appreciated the songs — words in tune. The songs were memorised and kept on repeating over and over again. His tantrums stopped when he heard the songs. His mother was too relieved to discover it. So she did not foresee that in public places her song therapy would not work. By now he got used to her 'voice that sang'. He threw up a tantrum when she spoke to him or to anybody else.

One day, he found that when her lips moved the song was heard. "The voices related to people and lips."

That looked easy. For a few days after that, he was in front of a mirror finding out a way to move his lips — pleading them to move in a silent way. But it did not flutter or move like mother's. All his image did was stare back. That was a terrible jolt. Another frustration and a great fear grew. He refused everything that belonged to 'the world'. He waited for some remarkable thing to happen and started to meditate for an answer.

Mother tried her best. She carried him on her back and danced across the rooms making funny faces and saying easy words like — "Ma, Baba" hoping he would say them after her. His father carried him and walked on the roads, as he refused to walk. "Can't recall why he refused to walk" — probably it was out of fear of the white shoes that mother got for him which squeaked. Her fault was none, as she wanted his walk to look cute and sound funny. But he was afraid, as the sound followed him every time he walked. That was not all.

Father had to take him through the same route. It was already frightening to go to new places and see new roads. He felt miserable when father stopped and stood while carrying him to talk to somebody.

I think about those dark days when mere sound of human voices annoyed him. Temper tantrums resulted, and lasted until he got exhausted.

"Why are you making the child weep?" a voice was directed to his father, also exhausted and nervous by the sudden outburst of the son, but he was too humble to answer back. He tried to hurry homewards. Several days later, mother discovered that he would have a fear if they tried a new route.

One day he was disturbed to find a different map of clouds overhead. It was a great disappointment, as he had memorised the previous day's sky.

A world full of improbabilities, racing towards uncertainty.

Mother joined her B.Ed. course, thinking about her future career as a teacher. She was about to complete two (years). The hope of staying with Dadu, his grandfather, and Dia, his grandmother, excited him. It would have been a very happy stay if he could have a fearless stay. Not that they did not love him but somehow he knew that mother was unwelcome.

Dadu was a person who always raised his voice when he spoke to mother. But he was very pleasant with him. Dia was moderate with her although she complained how tired she felt with her kitchen and grandson.

It was a brief stay of ten months and the message was received — "He had a bad mother."

She was bad because she studied. She was bad because Dia got tired. She was bad as she did her lesson plans when she was supposed to have played with him. She was bad, as the relatives thought that married women who were mothers should not study, neglecting their children. In a country where death is worshipped, where sacrifice is worshipped, where ambition is considered to be the key to greed and vice, she was bad.

He tried to side his mother mentally who was determined to finish her course and tried her way through. She got her appendix operated and then his endless journey to the various doctors began!

The first doctor he went to was an ENT [ear, nose and throat] specialist, who rang a bell to see how he reacted. He tapped his table, observed and prescribed a tonic or medicine called Encephabol, which the boy took for two months.

By then he had learnt a way to escape his uneasiness of lack of communication. It was masturbating on the edge of the bed or a sofa.

"Are you trying to swim?" His mother tried to reach out to her son and encouraged him by saying 'very good', at his every move. Hoping that he too would repeat after her and say at least something.

She hardly realised what her two and a half year old son was up to. It took her about a couple of weeks to find out and get worried. I can still remember her efforts to divert his attention by giving him books to see.

He waited for the next opportunity and started it again. The next time was when she was in college, and Dia was in the kitchen. The habit that he found irresistible to leave and got punished later for it.

But yes, he has developed a feeling of guilt and tries to think of something else when he is tempted.

*   *   *

I think about the times when he would change the environment around him, with the help of his imagination. He could go to places that did not exist, and they were like beautiful dreams.

One such was that of a staircase, which went high, higher and still higher reaching somewhere — anywhere. But a great disappointment occurred if it took him to nowhere and he had to start elevating again.

There was a funny hope that the staircase would lead him to God. The concept developed probably due to the fact that his Dia was a very pious lady and prayed a lot.

The obsession with staircases continued to exist even in the real world. One day in a doctor's chamber in Calcutta he spotted a staircase. He pushed and pulled his parents towards it. He refused anything else and thus got noticed by the people around. The parents had a tough time answering the inquisitive questions. Several attempts were made to calm him down without much effect.

A team of three doctors observed him and concluded that he had cerebral palsy.

There was another daydream that kept him occupied. It was that of a middle-aged gentleman sitting near him. It was very annoying to find that he sat everywhere and anywhere the boy turned. It took him years to find out that nobody else except him saw this man.

There were more things that puzzled him. There was a cloud on the chair and he found it difficult to sit on the chair. Sometimes the same person about whom mentioned before, sat on the chair.

I thought about his illusions and came to a satisfactory explanation. Probably in some magazine, or somewhere on the TV, he saw a similar person and thus imagined him anywhere.

It is important to mention that a time came when he lost control over these images that formed around him. He got lost in a situation that was unreal or super real. The chairs and tables were still there, but a book or a magazine or some eatables were seen in places where they were kept previously.

"I can see the past," thought the boy. He began to recall every sight, sound and smell — the happenings that had occurred around him and was glad to find out that he could replay the acts over and over again. In fact he could actually 'feel' the previous incidents around him.

"I can time travel," concluded the boy.

*

Nothing in the world is stable. It is very painful to see that what we love most, and consider as our own sometime or the other is to be given up, and is taken over by time. Then we sigh and tell ourselves — "Ah, that was once mine and I still miss it". I wonder whether it misses me too!

The boy, two and half years old was shocked to hear that his father had to move to a new house. He tried to show in his own way, how disappointed he was. It was painful.

Mother tried to practice her way, by taking him there, at least once a day, so that he could get used to the place and feel better and better about the house. But the boy cried louder and louder. The sorrow turned to anger. The parents were given every possible advice.

Some suggested that when children cried, a glass of water would help. Others suggested to feed him properly. A homeopathic medicine was also suggested that cured melancholic tendencies. Others blamed the 'cruelty' of the mother.

It was a terrible feeling to be in the new house. The toys looked so different and frightening that the boy stopped playing with them. He could not find any association between things that changed places.

It is something which I want to discuss in detail. It was a very fragmented world for the boy.

He could recognise the places first and then relate the objects to these places. A picture of a dog on the book could be identified as a dog, but a street dog could not be identified. It took years, and a lot of practice by him and the patience of his mother who kept on asking him questions, comparing pictures of a dog or a cow with the living beasts on the roads and the zoo, to overcome this. A book with the pictures of animals was their companion till he understood it.

The alphabet of different books too looked different. The things of a place looked different, the people also differed in real life from their photographs.

At times his friends have complained that he does not respond to them in public places or in markets. It is a thing of great embarrassment for them and the boy feels ashamed for it. Perhaps it would help to carry photographs of friends in the similar way as was done before.

Time was running out and the parents took the boy to a speech therapist. He was a bit impatient to handle a two years eleven months old boy and declared after ten minutes observation that he was sorry to say that the boy was mentally retarded.

I still go back to that moment and find that it was like a lightning striking down upon the family.

The mother staggered back to the hotel room, hugged her son and wept bitterly. The boy was sad too but could not show any feeling of pain. This is a major problem that the boy still faces. It needs to be mentioned that the boy had laughed at times when situations were sad. He wondered why he was not crying in a situation like that.

But had he spoken, he would have given a very touching speech about it. There was his mother weeping for a very uncertain future and there was the boy flapping with contentment. That was the last time he saw his mother so helpless, so afraid, so defeated.

The next thing that the boy found was that his mother was turning very religious. She started to believe in everything that was told to her. She began to keep fast on Fridays. She also asked the people and the neighbours what to do.

Somebody suggested that she take the boy to a temple, which had a healing aura around it. Other advised her to become a member of some religious organisation. The boy too began to think that one day there would be a miracle that would cure him.

A gentleman suggested that mother should separate rice from the grains before dawn. She should wrap them in a piece of white cloth, leave it on the road, taking care that nobody should see her. It took her the whole night to separate the required number of grains. That was a monsoon month and under a pouring sky, the white cloth was placed on the road — so that the boy spoke.

"Let us put him in a school," decided the parents. "He would socialise with other children and begin to talk."

So the boy went to the school, which was a congested drawing room of somebody's house. There were about twenty-five to thirty children sitting on a mat placed on the floor. The room was dark and the walls were painted dark green. The boy found it very funny to be there for the first ten days. Then he began to get bored of the place. He tried to show how much he disliked going there. But his mother had reasons for her determination. The boy was also no less stubborn. Every day he started to shout louder and louder on his way to school and at school.

"It will stop after some days," thought everybody. But the intensity of the three year one month old boys' voice was increasing every day, tiring out the patience of everyone.

"Sorry, he is not yet ready for a school," the mother was told by the teacher. Mother was not ready to give up. She asked whether she could bring him after a month. But the lady had enough of the boy. The boy too had enough of the school.

The boy was as stubborn as his mother was desperate and worried. She called the children of all age groups to play in her house, hoping that the boy would participate and try to interact with them. She distributed sweets liberally to make their house 'attractive' for the children.

Every evening they came home and played, while the boy tried to hide. What a noisy group! He was already disturbed by voices. He tried to flap away the sound with greater frequency.

I now regret the great opportunity that he lost! But there was a basic difficulty which the boy was facing. I have mentioned earlier that he had absolutely no control over his 'visions' and this happened whenever he was disturbed and found a situation difficult to cope with.

Had somebody asked him what a game was and had he the gift of speech, he would have defined it as 'a collective effort to follow some rules, and relax the mind.'

It was a very difficult task to imitate. That was a major drawback. It made him feel uneasy and probably he sheltered in the unreal world where the staircases took him higher and higher away from the voices, into silence.

The lonely self in the crowd. A contentment, aiming for liberation — a complete state of tranquility.

For my readers who are wondering why I called the boy 'stubborn' in the beginning and later became defensive about it, saying that he had a difficulty to imitate others.

He was obstinate because, when he was unable to play, it was believed to be his unwillingness to interact with children. So a popular belief developed that he was stubborn.

The gossiping hours of the ladies gave birth to special theories as to why the boy did not behave like other children. They fingered at mother and her ten months long B.Ed. course. Mother could never overcome her guilt and never appeared for her final exams. She still feels responsible for the boy's distortion.

There are always some people who like to be helpful. The boy's mother was supported by a friend of hers, Mrs Ray. "Bring him to my house after ten. You can finish off your work then."

In the evenings they both took the boy for a walk. Wherever the boy feared to go, they took him through those roads, ignoring his tantrums. Now mother was not alone to handle the child. She slowly gained back her confidence — with that her courage to tackle the questions and the pointed fingers.

A friend she has indeed! A big hearted Mrs Ray.

It was thought that a tricycle would be of much help to the boy. His sense of colour was great. So when it arrived, to show his appreciation for the tricycle, the boy arranged all his red toys in a line near it. It was red. (There was tough time ahead!)

"Now he can cycle on the road and forget the rules," the parents agreed. "Come on, son, sit and ride."

The boy sat, while the parents, took turns to push the cycle from behind. They giggled and argued about how long they should each push. One would have thought that it was they who got the tricycle! The boy sat passively without even trying to hold the handle, so that the person who was pushing from behind had to hold the handle too, in order to keep the cycle on the track. They soon got tired and the boy waited to be pushed.

After a few days, mother asked the boy to try the pedals. There was no response. "Come on son, try pushing your legs," she encouraged. "Yes son, push the pedals with your feet and chase me!"

I am afraid to mention how the look on her face that was so full of expectation was slowly changing to disappointment, then to anger and then to determination.

"Come on, move, and reach me, here is a benefit waiting for you!"

"Come on," the boy silently ordered his legs. The legs would not move and they both got worried and angry.

Yes, both mother and son were frustrated. She thought that her son was being stubborn and was unwilling to try. But she was determined.

"Drag the dog by the ear and teach it to bark when the door bell sounds."

She began to catch hold of his feet and push them over the pedals and dragged the pedals as she sat and walked backwards, complaining, and grumbling that her remarkable 'sparrow walk' in the backward direction would leave her with a crooked spine. She made the boy practice the cycling movement sitting on a chair whenever she got exhausted. By the end of the day, the boy was independently riding the tricycle.

> People, people all around
> Not a one to match,
> I search for a someone
> But I am a clown to watch!

That was understood by the three and half years old boy. He behaved in a way that gave a message saying — "Keep away, not your type!"

I wonder where the people get their good manners from. When somebody approaches the boy, and asks how he is, the boy feels good but also uncomfortable. The output of these feelings is that he runs away.

"That is rude," those near him point out. It was a worse show when he was three and half years old. His Dadu expired. He found that more than about the dead, people were talking about him — a living specimen to talk about.

His concerned mother was trying to stop him from getting up on the bed where the dead body was lying. His father was noting down the addresses of the various specialists about whom the 'mourners' spoke they knew of "Still there is time," they cautioned the puzzled father.

Now it was for him to decide when and where the boy should be taken. He wondered.

The boy wondered too — "why are people crowded around the bed? Let me get up and see!"

The more the boy was asked not to get up on the bed, the more stubborn he got. He was trying to find out why there were the flowers and garlands on and near the bed. The incense sticks were burning, making the bed look enchanted.

"They are worshipping him," thought the boy. "If I

sleep there, they will worship me too! They will stop asking questions about my speech!"

That was the birth of the first ambition to lie on the bed of flowers and incense sticks burning around.

Someone said that "he is on his way to eternal journey" and the boy wondered, "was this eternal journey like the flight of staircases — which he headed for whenever he felt trapped in the endless flow of happenings?"

The answer needed to be worked out. The climbing began. He believed that if he did that, he too would achieve death and have a bed like that. A way to get some respect. His parents would be freed too.

"Take him out from here," somebody asked his mother, who was battling with her son's efforts to sleep there.

There were a few who thought that "Poor boy, let him be there. He must have been very attached to his grandfather." The boy thought about the various attachments that he had and realised that there was nothing. All that he loved once — his old clothes, the house and toys were the cause of the sorrows he had.

"Even the personal thing like the body will die."

"I am the person, whose body is trapping the freedom that I seek," thought the boy.

He had seen what a remarkable thing death could do to a person. He becomes a hero and is talked about. The boy decided to work for it.

There was a total rejection to every attempt made to reach out to him. I remember that when the guests were still there, the boy woke up in the middle of the night and got upset to find that he was still alive. Instead of a bed of flowers, there was the ugly floor with a general bed. At least ten to twelve relatives were sleeping in the large room. The boy yelled and broke the peace of the night. With it, the whole house woke up. The mother was found guilty of not feeding in the boy well.

I can still recall her embarrassed apologies and her hurrying out of the room, to the courtyard, her humming a tune trying to calm him down, alone and afraid to sleep, lest the boy starts again to wake the people up.

The person who is so proud of herself was determined not to give them a second chance to get disturbed. The rest of the night saw a mother softly humming, and slowly walking up and down, carrying her child.

With a bitter sense of guilt for being unable to die, he finally gave up hope. But he refused to sleep on the floor with other people. They thought that the boy had cried the previous night because he wanted to sleep on the cot.

The changes that came to his thoughts after his Dadu passed away were significant. There was a total unwillingness to accept any thing.

His mother had taught him before, to do actions with

some nursery rhymes, which the boy loved to do. If anybody wonders "how a dumb mute boy could learn anything", I shall tell that "anybody can learn anything if one has the interest. More the interest, faster is the ability to learn."

Mother would sing 'Ba Ba Black Sheep' or 'Twinkle Twinkle little star' and he would do the actions. She was desperate to show that her child was not retarded before taking him to the next specialist. But with Dadu's death, he lost interest in these actions.

It looked absurd to exist. The boy refused to accept the existence of his body, and imagined himself to be a spirit.

Imagination took shape to lead his mind to a world of fantasies. By mere wishing he could feel that he was there. He believed that there was a world inside the mirror. He felt that the images were as real as the objects around him.

I am a spirit who can go there. The world certainly, is a better place in there, thought he. I am sure of the fact that he was with so much suffering that he wanted to escape there at any cost. By imagining himself as a spirit he could go there and feel the world.

It was as silent as he wished it to be. The people were not in a condition to use their voices, but they understood each other well. The children were also there. But they just thought. The people had the contentment of an abstract kind. Their eyes actually showed what each one thought. They reflect the staircases that the boy imagined.

The 'mirror travel' was a great way to be free of the noise around. The more he did the better he felt.

"God has sent me to your house to cure your son," the lady was determined to try something, while mother was thankful and delighted. The lady was determined to pray. She asked to show her the Pooja Room. Mother gladly took her there. The boy had a strange way of responding to strange objects and people. He sniffed them.

It happened so, that while the lady — very devoted — was praying and also impressing mother by shedding tears, the boy went and sniffed her.

"God is Great!" she announced. "He sure is great. My prayers are being heard. See how he came to me!"

Mother offered her fruits and sweets, as the lady said she had kept a fast for the sake of her son. Father came back from work and the lady hurried out, promising to return the next day.

Dear readers, you should like to know about the happenings that followed. On one side mother wanted her to continue the pray-way method. After all, the child went and kissed her. (They did not realise that the boy had actually sniffed.)

Father was determined to come back early the next day and tell the lady not to waste her time. Mother had a momentary mind at that time of crisis. She was and could be influenced by anybody. She was glad and thankful if anybody made decisions for her. But Father's words made sense to her.

"I will tell her," she decided, "a tough thing it would be, but the peace of the house is more important — specially at this time." Her voice was full of wisdom and assurance. She did not want him to get involved with it.

The lady had been very upset no doubt and went back the next day. She did not forget to tell that God would never forgive the mother.

The next week, an appointment was made with an Institute, which had a reputation of having some good child psychiatrists. The February or March of 1992 it was. The festival of Holi was celebrated by the neighbours. The boy was in no mood to join the other children. They had tried to persuade him to play. But he tried to be a spirit with no physical existence.

✳

The travel in the world of thoughts had increased. The imaginations took shape and form to a virtual existence of his self in that world.

My readers should not be guided by the idea that the boy had no "awareness" of the things that happened around him. He still appreciated a soothing voice, the advertisements in the television fascinated him.

He loved the white clouds in the blue sky, the wind that blew away the paper bits from his hands, the soft light of the dusk — and many more.

I do not want my readers to yawn at my list, which could be longer than the one I have given.

The main difficulty was that the boy was losing control over his body. A sense of denying its existence was so strong, that he could not respond to a situation the way it should have been done.

The boy cried less and showed more tolerance to the pains he got. His mother once mentioned to his father that she wondered why the boy did not make any fuss when he got hurt, like the other children did.

The boy wondered too. "But how should I make a fuss? I am the spirit, and above the reach of all pains — a free being," thought he.

I want to mention that once when the boy got hurt in the elbow, his mother had soothed his head, as the boy was not able to point the place where the pain was.

The boy went to the Institute where the clinical psychologist after studying him, told the parents that they had an 'AUTISTIC' son.

"It is a state when the child is so withdrawn that he is unable to understand what is going on around him."

"I understand very well," said the spirit in the boy.

"What should we do now?" asked the parents.

"Try to keep him busy," said the lady.

That month's task was to keep the boy busy and not letting him be alone. The next date of appointment was fixed after three weeks.

The parents searched the markets for some suitable toys that would keep the boy occupied for a long time.

There was a set of ten bowls big to small of different sizes. They had five different colours. Two bowls had identical colours. The boy had to keep them in such a way that a pillar could be made. The biggest was to be kept at the bottom and the rest to be arranged according to their sizes. The boy had also to match the identical colours — blue with blue and so on.

He loved it from the very beginning. It was like building his own staircase. The colours were so bright and so very interesting that the boy did not have to imagine about the dull staircase anymore. The first motivation he ever had!

His mother was so thrilled that she brought her camera, she took photographs of the boy building the pillar. They had of course a long way ahead, but the days were sure to be brighter. The boy needed more colours and materials to build the pillars. He surely wanted to be busy that way!

Sets of other building blocks were brought. The boy made pillars and staircases with them. The parents too joined in his game. That was the time when the boy stopped thinking about the staircase altogether. His mother taught him how two parallel pillars when joined by a bar at the top made a gate.

Soon, along with the pillars and gate, the boy was making zig zags also. He also learnt to make patterns with burnt matchsticks, for example rows of squares and crosses.

But he was not interested when they joined, head end to tail end to show him the 'train', arranging them in a line. The boy did not find that worth building.

Soon new sets of games were brought. One was 'Mixing Fixing'. The cavities with different shapes were there, and the boy had to fit into them blocks of exact shape. He learnt it fast, and improved his time with it.

He eagerly waited for new toys. The next game was a four piece jigsaw puzzle. The parents chose the pieces carefully, so as to keep the boy's interest going. It took no time for the boy to do it, and improve his time. He waited for the next game.

By the end of the third week, he was able to handle blocks, shapes and jigsaw puzzles of pieces eight in number. He went to the psychologist for the second time.

"I did not expect so much improvement in an autistic

child!" said the impressed lady. "He is not as severe as I had thought," she observed.

She assured the parents that if the child picked up at that rate, he had chances to be able to do much more.

The mother was so relieved that soon her son would be able to do more desirable things, that she began to lead a Spartan life. She got up at 4am, finished her bath and half her cooking and then prepared a 'goal' for the day. By seven the boy was up. After breakfast, the task began. There was no chance for the boy to get lost in his thoughts.

"Pick up the thing!"

If the boy tried to look away she hit him hard. That went on for days together. It worked. The boy became more attentive to her speech, and could follow her commands better. His father was unable to bear the sight, but he had great trust in his wife. So he went to another room without a comment.

The trouble came when the boy's Dia once visited her daughter. The boy as usual tried to look lost, and ignored his mother when she asked him to do something. Mother hit him hard which upset the grandmother. She thought that her daughter was the most cruel person and not worthy of being a mother.

The boy must admit that his mother has a remarkable resisting capacity. She could keep her voice very low and calm even if she got angry. The boy always felt secure with the soft pitch of her voice. She let Dia win in the vocal argument, but did her work.

"What are you looking at the calendar for?" asked the mother.

I must mention that the boy loved to watch the different calendars of different rooms and then recall the numbers. He also compared them. He thus spent a lot of time, gazing at the numbers. He wanted to know what they meant. He found a kind of pattern in them. He wondered how the figures bent and straightened up, curled and sometimes broke!

Later he came to know that the straight line was number one, broken ones were number four and seven, while the curled figure was number six.

Many times, the boy wondered whether they were like pieces of strings, which would straighten up or curl up. He laughed at the thought while other wondered.

"Should we see the calendar?" The mother asked the boy. She put him to her left side and began reading the numbers. Then she copied them in bright colours, on a separate page, letting the boy compare the shapes. She pointed at a number that she had written, for example 14. The boy had to find it on the calendar. When she was satisfied, she asked him to point at number 14, all by himself — which the boy was able to do.

Surprised and encouraged, she asked him all the other numbers one by one. The boy was too eager to show. The mother was so pleased to find the new ability of her son, that she called her next door neighbour to tell her about it. "He can identify the numbers!" she said to the lady, who was not at all interested. The air balloon inside the mother contracted immediately.

People love to take special interests in the 'cannots' and not the 'cans'.

10th of April 1992 it was. There was a kind of celebration in the family of three. The parents began to dream about the better times ahead. The boy formed loops, lines and circles called sixes, ones and zeros in his mind. The difference was that he knew what they were called. Next day, he learnt to recognise the numbers till hundred.

The boy pointed out to a number as his mother called out a particular number from the jumbled group.

"He is doing it consistently," mother informed the boy's father who was so anxious that he kept calling home every half an hour's interval to get the latest information.

The boy was so interested that he was ready to learn more. He was ready for the New World that was in front of him. The puzzles and games — making pillars and building staircases — were also to be done.

But the boy waited for the numbers to be taught again. Mother wanted to try out the alphabets in the same way. They were learnt fast as usual. The boy knew by the end of the day that he had a wonderful memory — something to be proud of.

He reasoned out that he might give it a try to be a 'body' instead of a 'spirit'. But that was not any easy work.

He felt that his body was scattered and it was difficult to collect it together. He saw himself as a hand or as a leg and would turn around to assemble his parts to the whole.

He spun round and round to be faster than the fan. He felt so that way!

He got the idea of spinning from the fan as he saw that its blades that were otherwise separate joined together to a complete circle, when they turned in speed.

The boy went to an ecstasy as he rotated himself faster and faster.

If anybody tried to stop him he felt scattered again.

A new environment became very difficult to cope with, as he felt that he was not able to find his body. Only if he ran fast or flapped his hands he was able to find his presence.

The helplessness of a scattered self was to taunt him for years together — even as I write this page.

That projected the boy as a total weird personality and instead of getting respect for his 'have's', he gets the curious looks or 'sympathies' from the strangers.

But as I was continuing with the eventful month of April 1992, the topic should not be interrupted by the weirdness of a mental delusion.

That week brought the dawn of hope to the parents, and the boy too found an interest to communicate.

For at the end of the week, he not only could count and add, but also could read and spell by pointing out from the board in which his mother had written down the alphabets using bright colours.

"Once upon a time, there was a crow," mother began her story. She drew a crow on a page. The boy loved colours. Although the crow was black, she made the words she wrote look colourful and bright. She began her first lesson through the story about the 'thirsty crow'. It was a well planned lesson.

The boy could actually feel the heat of the midday sun and the dry landscape. The crow became his favourite bird. Black became his favourite colour for a while. He could 'feel' the variety of other colours mocking the darkness of the black.

The boy saw the darkness of the night revealing the universe in the sky, while the brightness of the day shading the real sky with its colours so that the stars could not be seen. But again he got confused. If darkness revealed all, why was that, if he went to a dark room, things got difficult to be

identified? He was puzzled and started to go to some dark corner and think about 'black'.

But do not be afraid readers — I shall not prolong my dark-affinity any longer. Let it be buried in its own darkness.

If I told you that the boy for a while felt that life was worth living because he found everything around had a life and had a lesson to teach, then my dear readers — you would think that it is a crazy thought. But as this boy got interest in the words and numbers, he made stories with them.

For example, number one was very proud to be above all the numbers. Number two continued in that if it was not careful, it could slip and fall as the two had a curled head over which one had to balance with one leg. In reply number one said "only the hard workers are number one."

The boy saw a chair as a living lady ready to comfort the tired, the cupboard as a big-mouthed person, ready to eat anything you feed.

"What makes you laugh?" asked mother. The boy laughed more, imagining the letters that formed the word "goat" were in dispute, each one making its own phonetic sound — a resulting noise that was different from the way "goat" sounded.

So the boy made a new game. He had learnt already how to read. He thought about different words and made the letters argue and talk. He tried to make a resulting sound.

Mother was alert to any noise that the boy made — only distorted sound. The specialist had warned her that autistics have the tendency to form a word that occasionally made no sense at all.

The boy was making every possible sound — imagining the letters of words making dialogues.

To check that she put him to more tasks and joined him in making zig zags, for example, or teaching him.

I do not know about other cases who have the similar problem, but I should suggest to all their guardians to discourage the meaningless babblings that they tend to do after the age of three, as it gets out of control.

Being mute is better than distortion.

*

Our instincts are very sensitive to differences, specially if it involves a different behaviour. Some people were interested in the boy for his distorted behaviour, more interested in the 'have nots' rather than the abilities that he had.

Some, yes, said that they were impressed. But there were others who were a bit sceptical as to "how a boy who can't talk, can calculate or communicate."

The boy wondered about the different thoughts that the people had and behaved accordingly. For them, who trusted him, he was eager to communicate, but for those who were sceptics, he refused to co-operate.

I am perhaps diverting away, dear readers, from my point, but as I go back in time, I find the boy at the specialist's office, and also answering the IQ test questions by pointing on the board. He was proud to see the admiration on her face. It was a pleasure to be understood as a boy who was better in intelligence, than other of his own age.

'But' my dear readers. I repeat the word 'but' again. The boy was still an intelligent junk, not functioning in the useful way.

Another three months passed with the intelligence tests and the parents realised that the Institute had nothing else to contribute to the further improvement.

They took him to a paediatrician who measured his head and prescribed a dose for the boy, a medicine that would check his hyperactivity. The boy took the first dose and began to feel numb. "His eyes are still and he is not walking properly," said the alarmed mother. She was loud, but the boy heard her voice faintly. He heard other sounds also — faintly. It was alarming, and the boy feared.

The parents decided not to continue with the medicine. By evening the numbness was gone and sounds got louder again.

The year 1992 was about to close, and the winter was at the door. The parents were wondering where next to take the boy.

They decided to take him to a reputed hospital — The Christian Medical College Hospital [CMCH] in Vellore. But they had to go through several hurdles of permissions — permissions from people who authorise the various government sanctions in the medical field at his father's company. It so happens that the company is under the Government of India, providing all the facilities to the employees. It also has a small hospital with a few beds, a handful of doctors and many rules.

"Can you treat him?" asked the father to the Chief Medical Officer. He was reluctant to refer the boy to the suggested hospital (CMCH, Vellore) in the interest of the company. So he referred the boy's case to another hospital close by (The Tata Main Hospital in Jamshedpur).

"Don't worry. I will help you get referred from there to the desired hospital," (Vellore) said the lady who was the wife of an influential authority of the company.

The doctors there were seldom on time. They made a special air of 'born to rule' aura around them. People waited outside every chamber bored but patient. The boy was not patient. He tried to walk on the corridors, and then had to be pulled back by one of the parents.

After a long while, the doctors of the psychiatry section arrived. The boy went in with a lot of hope that he would be appreciated for his communication skills and computing abilities. But that could not impress them. They forwarded the case to the scanning section.

"Why can't you refer him to the Hospital where facilities are available?" (CMCH, Vellore) asked the impatient father. But the air of confidence around the doctors replied back — "Why should we?" "He is a case for you, but he is our son," argued the mother. But doctors have the power.

The lady I mentioned earlier reassured the parents to hold their patience. She would talk to an authority of the Hospital and get the case forwarded.

Patients are helpless to the whims of doctors. The CAT scanning was unavoidable and the parents took the boy to the scanning section. The parents were not against scanning, but wanted it to be done at the better place, which has a reputation of experienced neurologists.

The room was big and full of instruments. The boy was asked to lie down on the narrow bed that began to move as soon as he did so. He was terrified to find himself moving towards the round window.

"I won't let it happen," he decided and jumped out of the moving bed. The boy was chased around the room and caught. He was put back to the bed and was held by the limbs by at least four people. But the head shook in protest. The doctor in charge decided to sedate him. The boy was alert. He did understand that it was a way to put him back inside the round window.

The nurse injected him with a dose of sedative and the boy was expected to sleep.

"But I won't let myself sleep to be inside the round window," decided the boy and battled with his drowsiness. The will power proved stronger than the chemical, at least for an hour. There were other cases to be taken care of and the doctor asked the parents to fix up an appointment for some later date. The boy on the way back home gave up to sedation, and slept for hours together. There was no round window to be afraid of.

The father was introduced by the lady about whom I had mentioned before to an authority of the Hospital. He realised how important time mattered to the parents and to the boy.

So, with a stroke of his pen, he referred the boy to the much-awaited Hospital.

Good Samaritans are there,
But on the earth rare!

✶

"Today you tell me a story," requested Mother, as the boy sat with the board to communicate. The boy had just heard the stories from Aesop's Fables, and made up a story about a goat which had been disobedient and ran far away from home, losing its way back, finally searched and found by its mother. The story was the first effort to put his imaginations into words. The boy's mother was proud, surprised and encouraged. The boy was happy too, as he found that he had another ability to be proud of. She read and reread it, with and without audience. The boy heard it and wondered about his next story.

The same way, about fifteen more stories were told.

The train journey to South India was long and full of happenings. The parents had a tough time to cope with the boy's rules, which made him get upset and panic at anything that he felt was unusual.

For example, whenever the train stopped in the middle, he got upset and created a lot of discomfort to the people around by crying loudly. He got upset every time he saw a particular person, passing by his seat. He threw a tantrum when the direction of the train changed after Vishakhapatnam. He cried with fear thinking that they were probably going back.

There were curious looks and suggestions from people, many of whom were patients themselves, heading for the same destiny. The train reached the station after two long days.

The hospital was a place of hope as the patients suffered less due to the vocal touches given by the doctors and the human-like way they heard the complaints of each patient. The patients had faith in the doctors and looked up to them next to God. Doctors did not make the patients wait and waste time.

The boy was taken to the neurology section. The doctors were surprised at the ability of the boy regarding his skills.

They asked him to point at his body parts, but the boy could not do it. Not that he was ignorant of the parts of the human body, but he was unable to point and identify them in his own self. Pointing at objects was difficult too, as he pointed only at the letters on the board and could not generalise it with the other things. Then the doctors asked the other way round. They touched his legs and hands and so on. They asked him to point on the board. This he did with ease.

The doctors wanted to do his EEG and scanning the next day. The boy was already aware of the words, and knew what was in the store. The round window was here too! But he decided to fight it. The next day he tried to be sick. He vomited in the morning. He was nervous and did not want to be sedated.

His earlier experience of sedation was bad, and the very thought of it made him nauseate. However he was given the injection but he fought with his drowsiness. The doctor asked the parents to take him back to the hotel and bring him back as soon as he slept.

The boy heard it, and he heard it well. He slept after returning to the hotel. As soon as his father tried to carry him back, he opened his eyes and was put back to bed by the cautious father. The parents tried again and again and finally gave up. They carried the boy back to the doctor, for him to decide what to be done.

I should clarify that the sedative had caused so much numbness, that the boy was not able to walk or even lift up his head. But occasionally he gave a groan of irritation to prove that he was not at all asleep. Moreover, he felt uneasy without a bed. The doctor decided to sedate him slowly and he was admitted to the neurology ward.

*

It was a stay for about a week in the three-bedded room of the ward. The doctors were keeping a close observation of him. But the boy enjoyed it, as he was being treated like a guest of honour. The nurses too brought him some toys to play with. The doctors asked him questions and the boy answered them by pointing on the board. He was enjoying the stay thoroughly.

"Why don't you talk," asked a doctor. The boy pointed that he did not like to speak. That was what some people believed, and the boy thought, perhaps that was a reason for his silence.

He was rather beginning to enjoy his silence. What better could be a way to enjoy such attention!

But gradually he began to hate the high ceilings and the green curtains of the hospital ward. He began to feel dizzy and nauseate. That may have been due to the sedative or that constant smell of medicine around the place. The walls were white and it remained to be a colour of sickness for the boy.

The doctors had instructed the nurses in charge to get his EEG and scanning done, as soon as he sleeps.

Finally to everybody's relief he slept, and he slept, and let the medical way to proceed.

He was kept there for a few days more for an IQ test, which was held in the Mental Health Centre called Bagayam. He was confident with himself and scored very high. He got proud of his worthless worth.

Was he not a riddle for all those men and their

profession? Was he not a wise dumb? So he compared himself to a filled vessel that made less sound, thinking of the proverb 'empty vessel sounds much'.

What was in the report of the scanning and EEG is least of my concern. But for the concerned well wishers, I must say that the boy had 'normal' wha. . . . ? He was discharged from the neurology ward and forwarded to the psychiatry section.

There was a week's gap, and the parents went to visit a relative living in Bangalore and then see a part of South India.

The boy was too much flattered by the remarkable impact he made on the people who wondered how he possessed such gift.

"He is a great soul," said somebody. The boy also wondered about the greatness that he had, and aimed to be greater. He spoke of wisdom, as it was easy and it made him popular. He was encouraged by the questions like what reality of God was.

He confidently replied that "All that we feel through our senses, and those that existed beyond our senses, the attitudes and appreciations through which we receive our stimulations is God."

Somebody noted it down.

"What is heaven?" Somebody asked the boy and he pointed that, "It is a state of ultimate joy and happiness." Somebody wrote it down as golden words.

The boy waited for the next questions and he eagerly waited. The holidays came to an end. They went back to the hospital.

The next day, the boy was admitted to the Mental Hospital.

He hated the place. The place had too much openness. Openness disturbed him as he felt his body being scattered. He could not bear it, and started throwing tantrums out of fear.

The fear of open spaces disturbed him and continued to haunt him for years. Still the boy loved the yellow flowers that fell from the big trees making the paths bright.

He was a lover of regulations. Walking on the road was easier than walking on the fields. He hated places that were full of freedom and got hyperactive.

The more awkward he became, the more suspicious the psychiatrist became regarding his intelligence. They suspected that the mother was trying to play up a trick. "I came here to find help for my son and not to show you any magic," replied the mother, angry and worried.

She was worried. "It is the right place for his treatment?" she asked her husband, as they saw their son solving the jigsaw puzzle. The boy had never felt so restless before. He tried to think of the staircase and the wonderful world of silence, which he used to imagine. But he could not concentrate as he used to.

This was because of education, which had opened a new world for him. He was frustrated for not being able to be on the imagined staircases. He got angry with mother for educating him. Many a time when he tries to get a feeling of bliss, by imagining fantasies, his knowledge about the subject prevents him to dive into the virtual. It was irritating. He could not 'feel' the virtual as he did before.

For instance, he wanted to change the colour of the surroundings to black and shades of darkness. But soon, at least ten things which mother had taught about black came to his mind, and prevented his vision.

(1) Black is the absorber of light

(2) Black is the good conductor of heat

(3) Black of our hair is due to melatin

(4) Black sky of the night

(5) Black sheep calling Ba-Ba

(6) Black hole of the Cosmos

(7) Black box of the aeroplane

(8) Black Sea

(9) Black Negro

(10) Black Cotton soil

With these things disturbing him, he could not create the world with black.

He started making a continuous clicking sound, with his tongue. It made the doctors conclude "that he had autism of a 'moderate level'." There was no use of teaching him, as he may not be able to write.

Mother was very upset. But she gets the brightest ideas when she is under strain. "Necessity is the mother of invention" she boasts.

She noted down all the points that made him autistic. Eye contact problem, unable to point at objects. The boy led somebody by the hand to get some object. He could not use any gestures or express his feelings. He was hyperactive, could not imitate, and many more drawbacks that made the boy get the label.

"But he has a language also, in fact three languages," argued the mother.

"He can't write," reassured the doctors.

Mother started her task the next day. She took the boy's hand and made a pointing posture with it. She kept a few objects like a book, a glass, a shirt and other common things. "As you do with the alphabet, show me the objects I name."

A difficulty was developing when the object was kept behind him, as he could not turn and point.

Now it was 'her' turn to throw a tantrum!

The boy needed time for the ability like that. The mother understood that there was too much pressure on the child. The cloud of uncertainty was fast approaching the family. Mother said she would not accept the fact that there was no 'use' teaching the boy, and she was certain that with right motivation he would be able to write also.

Father was depressed too. Whatever the doctors told him was discouraging. The boy had never seen his parents argue so much.

But they were to stay there for 'occupational therapy', for the next one and half month. This therapy was attended by mental patients of adult age group. The room was big and had chairs for big men and women. It needs to be mentioned that the boy was unable to sit on a chair with his legs hanging loose. The therapist tried to make him sit using force. But the boy just ran around the room — around the chairs and long tables. Of course, one thing interested him — the pack of cards which the people played in the afternoon. But they gave him beads to thread. That made a boring time waste for the boy.

There was a school for the mentally retarded children,

which the boy attended in the morning. It had some interesting puzzles and games. They were new, as other children were not able to use them.

He spent the afternoons running around the tables of the therapy room. No one except his mother tried to stop him. She was worried for the increasing hyperactivity of the boy.

I must say that the boy too felt insecure, and rejected every ability that once he was proud to display. He refused to communicate.

The board communication after all was not considered to be valid, and he was not communicating with others when his mother was not holding the board that was a big and a serious problem.

For many a times, he could not be used to someone else holding the board. The problem was that he needed time to get used to the person — his touch and most important — his voice. The voice problem was due to the fact that words were told differently by different individuals. It needed to be rectified through gradual exposure to people — and being conditioned to reply to voices that questioned.

To my readers who may get tired of my theories and are impatiently waiting for "Then what happened?" I must say that the boy also underwent an ENT term, from where he was sent to All India Institute of Speech and Hearing.

The parents took the boy on the wrong day. Saturday was not a working day. So they decided to wait till Monday.

Monday was a busy day. The boy's case was registered at the Institute. Since he did not co-operate with the hearing ability test, he was sent to the psychology section for evaluation.

The two clinical psychologists who saw him, ignored the fact that he had a way to communicate by pointing and forming words from the alphabet.

"Did he have any IQ test before?" they asked the parents. The father showed the papers from the Vellore where the boy got a 'genius' 0 grade.

"We don't accept it. The test result may say something else here!"

The parents thought it was a waste of time, as the IQ tests which the boy had undergone before had nothing to do with his speech or behaviour.

The boy was then introduced to Dr Prathibha Karanth. For a while the boy was held spell-bound, when he entered the room. Behind the table sat a smiling lady, not with the usual look of the 'all knowing doctor', which the boy had expected. But soon he found another attractive thing. It was a table calendar, with sketches of old buildings in the pages. He liked it, he picked up and he held it. Mother tried to stop him by taking it from his hand and putting it back to its place.

"Let him have it," said the lady with a generous smile. "But ask him why he likes it so much".

That puzzled the boy. "Why do I like it?" he asked him-self. A question that was of a totally new kind — nobody had asked him anything similar before. But an answer was being expected. He pointed out at the alphabet and replied that "I like its colour contrast". That was not a very honest answer. But it made the boy escape other questions.

In fact, no other specialist had directed a question, which kept him searching for the answer. There were more questions waiting for the boy from her, in the later months to come.

Two months later, he was to come back to Mysore. The two months gap was very crucial for the boy as he learnt how to write. That was yet another story.

As I had mentioned before, that people were sceptic about the boy's abilities, his mother insisted that he should write. She brought him a pencil and a paper. She drew a line. The boy showed reluctance to hold the pencil. Any new activ-ity terrified him. He kept his grip on the pencil so loose that every time his mother gave it to him, he dropped it.

You can drag the horse to the water, but you can not make it drink. But mother was equally stubborn. She tied the pencil to his hand with a rubber band, so that he could not shake it off. She kept him sitting at the same place, until he drew the lines. By the end of the day, the boy was drawing not only horizontal lines, but vertical lines too. A notebook was given to him and he soon filled it up with lines. But there was more to be done.

He needed to move onwards. He needed to write.

The next thing that his mother did was to paste pictures from magazines. She insisted that the boy should point on the board of the alphabet first and answer questions, then write the answer by copying the alphabet which he pointed.

The problem was seen. He was unable to copy and mother was throwing up a tantrum. She was not ready to give up.

"Let me hold your shoulder like I used to when you started pointing and communicating," she said, trying to find a way.

This time it was easy for the boy to write, as he could feel the presence of the hand, his own hand linked to his body, at the shoulder point, where his mother was holding him.

I have a concrete proof that to start with any new activity, it is important for the autistics like the boy, to be held at that part of the body, which does the work as the 'relating' ability develops slowly through practice. Then it can be faded out as the person gets the habit of that particular work.

The boy could relate his thoughts to words and express them by pointing or writing only when somebody held his shoulder.

July end he went to Mysore, and started undergoing 'speech therapy'. Dr Prathibha Karanth began her treatment not as a doctor but as his 'Kaki' which meant 'Aunty'. The boy was to be a special person — a capable human being and not a person labelled as autistic, with certain expected behaviour patterns.

The parents were too willing to try the treatment under her, as they got much hope.

The first few days were spent in questions and answers. She wrote the questions like "Why don't you talk?" The boy replied that "You won't understand". The lady was not to be satisfied with that and kept up the enquiry by stating that "I want to understand if you explain it better." The boy said that "I hear the sound of 'oum' so much, that other sounds get lost".

It was not a very dishonest reply as he imagined to hear a constant hum that kept him occupied whenever he felt like switching off. But it was also meant to impress the lady. But she proved to be a hard nut to crack. She asked more questions, saying that she was an agnostic, and he needed to find a better reason than that. What reason could the boy who wanted to talk but did not know to talk, give?

So he wrote to her that "being autistic I have every right to be unable to talk". Then, to close the matter, he placed his hand on the page and traced it.

The lady showed no impatience.

The boy's mother was advised by some people that there was a 'Holy Lady' who cured anybody whom even doctors could not cure. The bus was to leave for that place the next evening. If she wished, she could join the devotees.

She was more than willing and bought two tickets for the pilgrimage to the healer. A quick solution for the big problem was aspired, and the blessings of the lady were obtained. But they returned with no solution. The boy continued to flap and remained mute. For the fifth time she promised herself not to be carried away. Of course the promise was short lived, and two weeks later she visited a Godman.

What a faith she had! Each time she had a fresh hope, she prayed harder.

The boy felt very guilty about the whole matter. He lost every hope, when he saw his otherwise strong mother submitting to these people. He wanted her to be the fearless self as she otherwise is. He felt confident when she was confident.

His Kaki solved the problem. She happened to influence her a great deal. One day, she asked her to put the question to the boy "what he felt about these men" and the boy replied that he had no faith and was disappointed every time he came back, without speech.

Mother too defended herself by saying that at times her patience gets lost and she hopes for some quick solution.

If she hurt the sentiments of the boy, she was sorry. But all along she meant well and she would not go to any more such places, as she was aware of her son's feelings. She kept her word till date.

Kaki saw him everyday for an hour and the boy responded very less during the two months stay. He spent time by tracing his hands on the pages she gave. But he enjoyed her presence.

The therapist who dealt with his speech was Roopa Rao. She had a great face and a very warm smile. The boy had a wonderful sensation when she sat near him. He began to eagerly wait for her sessions. It was a totally different experience for him. He had a remarkable ability to compose verses.

He wrote for her

> Burning quietly in the heart
> Where quiet emotions lay
> My love burnt with so strong glow,
> The reason perhaps I can't say.

Mother reacted to it in a very mixed way. She was amazed and nervous too. She was not ready to accept that her five year old son was able to write lines to pay his compliments to someone.

She ran to his Kaki to inform her about it, and ask her, whether she would encourage him further.

Kaki told her not to be worried as the words were harmless, and did not hurt anybody. The boy wrote another verse similar to it the next day

> My love is like a deep sea,
> Seen by all as blue,

Only those who know of it
Sees its real view.

    The boy had found a subject to write. He aimed to write for ladies as they appreciated his verses most. He wished to gift them the words of appreciation. All he needed was to make them personal, and add the tools of external beauty to their lines.

I saw her sparkling lines
Dark as night they glowed —
When I closely looked at them.
I saw my own shadow.

Beauty kissed her feet gently
Laughter filled her face,
Her warming smile reached my heart
My heart was set ablaze.

Two months stay in Mysore ended with a transition in the outlook of the boy. He began to feel more respectable and feel more sure about himself. He wanted to see his writing as a mode to be respected. He needed to learn more.

His mother read out to him the following books — The Land of Oz, The Hunchback of Notre Dame, and Treasure Island.

Returning to the township was not easy for the boy. He felt trapped in the silence of the place. He felt idle, and started a few rituals like touching certain objects in a particular way, so that if anybody stopped or interrupted him, he got upset, angry and then furious. His temper tantrums also started for this fresh cause, which was irritability. He had lost the ability to dream of the staircases altogether and panicked.

On the roads, he wanted to hold the lands of his parents in a particular way.

I can not recall why this was so, but he felt very insecure without the rituals as he felt his presence through them. It seemed impossible to stop.

The parents decided to return to Mysore, as the situation was getting out of control. When they went back to Mysore, they hoped to stay there for at least four months. The father would go back after a week and the boy's mother would continue to stay.

A family whom they had met before during their earlier

stay in Mysore, offered to host them as their paying guest. The lady was Dr Mallika, and the gentleman was Mr Raghu. They were so impressed by the boy's writings that they refused to accept any guest charges at first, but the parents insisted. They would find the stay 'uncomfortable', if they were to stay free of cost.

The boy came to Mysore for fresh speech therapy in the month of December '93 with several behaviour problems, the major being temper tantrums, resulting from 'irritability'. The anger due to change in routine, change in the paths, change in bus routes, change in the position while walking or sitting, turned to temper tantrums and they took hours to stop.

His mother was the usual victim as the people asked her why her son was crying. Although she knew that the boy was crying for the change in her position of walking which the boy wanted. He wanted her to walk by his right, while she was determined to walk by his left to show him that she was more stubborn.

But this explanation would be complicated for a person who did not know anything of autism, to be satisfied, as an answer to his concerned question "Why is he crying?"

"He wants another ice cream," came the mother's prompt reply, and further questions were thus avoided.

The boy had a problem to associate his reasons with his actions. He was aware of his mind working but not aware of his body acting.

The therapy sessions with his Kaki helped him. He could feel his action better inside her room, as he squatted on the mat, kept on the floor. He felt better as she sat on the floor with him and gave him a piece of paper to scribble. He drew arrows, houses and traced his palm. She conversed with him. It was a one-sided speech but the boy was getting to feel his actions as he tried to pull the pencils or the biscuits from her hand. He became used to a new ritual, of removing his shoes after entering her room and then racing to the toilet.

This he did to concentrate better. He felt so this way as he believed that going to the toilet was a way to start anything.

He began and ended the day by going to the toilet, he began and ended his journeys by going to the toilet. So why not his therapy sessions?

The speech therapist who was working with him was Deepa Bhat. She had a 'matter of fact' way of talking, and was willing to work not for herself, but for her 'case'. She looked energetic and had strong bones in her thin long hands. She had the ability to pull the boy inside the therapy rooms, when the boy felt and acted stubborn by stiffening up his body.

"I want to talk to Kaki," the boy felt after a few weeks of therapy. It was at first, not a very strong wish, but the desire to talk to her was growing.

Deepa forced him to communicate by pointing on the board. It was after several days attempt that the boy used her hands' support to communicate.

She asked him several types of questions about his parents and of course why he did not speak. The boy was a bit puzzled, as he himself had no answer as to why he did not speak.

He just felt he knew that he was a reincarnation of some great being as he heard other people say so. He wondered who could he had been.

Then he felt may be the arguments that took place between his parents were the cause of his inability to speak. Deepa thought it best to consult the matter with Dr Karanth. The boy felt may be, if he would discuss the matter with her, he would be able to speak. He tried to recall some unpleasant times when his parents had argued about his treatment, and added colours to them. He hoped to get his speech after showing his bitterness.

Kaki trusted every bit of the story he told and spoke to the parents separately.

The boy had thought that if he spoke about his bitterness to Kaki, his speech would come. He was so sure of it, that he imagined that picture of a very disturbed family, and was able to convince Kaki how threatened he felt when they argued. He was also expecting them to fight, after Kaki spoke to them.

By seeing them fight, he thought, he would find the real reason for his not being able to talk. But they did not fight or blame each other. Instead, they told him that it was after his problems started, that they began to argue over his 'complexities in behaviour', resulting from the guilt of not parenting him well. They told him that they felt socially distanced because of him.

The boy then thought that perhaps if his father played with him, his speech would come faster. He had a belief that speech 'comes' to the children when they play, they do not need to try for it, as he watched the playing children with speech.

Kaki gave him extra hours at the Institute and also at her home. The boy felt good, but speech was yet to come. Deepa too was giving her 'revision' time for him, as she was the medium of communication with Kaki. She spent hours with him to find exactly what worried him. The boy wondered too.

His father had already started playing with him by taking two months' leave from work. The boy waited for speech to come, as he ran with him and played catch and chase. That was the only game he knew how to play, although mentally he knew about other games.

I would like to discuss this. As I have mentioned before, the knowledge and the application of the knowledge were like the two ends of a string, which were distinctly separated by a distance called 'relation'. So, although, he knew that balls could be caught or hit with a bat or could be kicked, he could not 'use' the ball.

The catch and chase game was also having a problem for

the boy, as he could not chase anybody, though he enjoyed somebody chasing him and gave a running and dodging game to the person who chased him. The difficulty was overcome, when his mother held a biscuit in her hand and taught the boy how to chase the 'person', by slowly fading the biscuit.

This I mentioned because, the other day I was watching another autistic boy who was dodging around a tree when his mother was trying to chase him. She was in a hurry to go. But the boy was conveying the message that he was in the mood to be chased and 'feel' the use of his body.

It is a common problem? I am yet to know.

The first thing that was decided was to continue their stay for a longer time in Mysore. His father was searching for a job of some suitable kind that required his experience.

Though the parents changed their residence to a rented place, and set up a home away from home, yet they shared a common dream of going back to their home, to 'live happily ever after'.

But the boy was afraid to go back. He had some of his bitter experiences in that place. He told himself that he would not let them take them back.

The next problem which he thought he had, was his mother teaching him. He told Kaki about it, thinking that if he went back, his mother would teach him there.

I want to confess on behalf of the boy to his mother, as he was putting her in a very cornered situation of not mothering him well.

"She is more of a teacher than a mother," he said.

I realise how shocked she must have felt after hearing about it.

The books were kept away and the boy was allowed to spend the time the way he wanted to.

So his father came to the Speech Institute and played with him — catch and chase. He got tired after sometime, and they sat on a bench of the 'Therapy Park'.

The boy began to miss his lessons with his mother.

Meanwhile, the sessions with Deepa were coming to an end. He began to feel very miserable, as he would miss her.

> Time you bring things to us
> And moments so fresh and good,
> Then take away the moments of love.
> For reasons not understood.
> The pain of loss at time of part
> Is like a broken pot,
> That he was proud of its glaze
> But now left to rot.

Deepa left in the month of June. Shantala began her therapy. The boy would ever be grateful to her, as she taught him how to dress and eat. She did it step by step taking a lot of patience. She had a very calm approach and a soft voice. By the end of the second month, the boy could eat and dress himself. The hands had better use other than flapping! He could 'feel' his hands better.

The same month mother taught him colouring. That born teacher could never keep herself away from teaching. In fact, the boy was also missing his lessons with her. The colouring books were bought, and he had to colour the pictures exactly the way in which the sample drawings were coloured.

The time was spent with sketch pens and colour pencils. The boy was able to colour better and better every day. He sat with them for long hours. At first, he coloured for the sake of keeping himself occupied, but slowly, he began to enjoy the activity.

He was eager to finish colouring one book as mother bought him the next one as soon as he finished it. Then he learnt tracing and copying.

It is a common problem to copy figures for many of the autistics, as I have heard and experienced. But I am not saying it with any authority, as there are experts, who have far better information in the field. So, my observation and statement is based on my own observation and experience.

The boy found great difficulty in copying out figures like a circle or a square. Mother had to hold his hands and make him draw the figures, as the boy was slowly beginning to understand 'how' to do it.

I repeat 'how' to do it and not what to do. My readers must not have the impression that he did not know what to do, but it was 'how' to do. In fact every problem that he faced was due to this 'how'.

How shall I play!
Can't you talk?
How shall I talk!
Can't you listen to us?
How shall I listen to you!
Will you try?
Yes, I will try, but teach me how to try.

Mother got the point and panicked. "How shall I teach you how to try?" she asked her son helplessly.

Kaki was required to think of a way to let the boy learn 'how to try'. He was asked to learn imitating others first.

The speech therapist was instructed to teach the boy the basic actions through some free-hand exercises that are easy for children to learn.

"One," the therapist called Anil said, and raised his hands parallel to each other. The boy had to imitate him.

"Two," he said and brought them forward. The boy thought it worth trying and waited for 'three' and 'four'.

"So this is what they called trying was," the boy concluded. "The wanting to do an activity by using your body."

My readers must be tired of the phrases 'using the body', and 'feeling the body', since I repeatedly use them. But that is unavoidable as I explain every stage of learning and coping with the confusion of relating the mind and body. The constant guilt of not being able to be a proper and normal human being, was there too, standing in his way to 'try' and be like others.

The exercises continued. It was better than playing games, as it was more 'organised' than games. In free hand exercises, the actions were structured as the numbers one, two and so on. The boy knew his next move. But games were unpredictable, uncertain, confusing and difficult.

It was in the same month when mother taught him how to catch a ball. She made him stand very close to her and started to play 'give and take' game with the ball. When the boy was told to give the ball, he placed it on mother's hand. She immediately gave it back to him.

The boy could concentrate better and better in the activity with practice and repetition. When she was satisfied with his concentration, she slowly began to step backwards and instead of placing the ball in his hand, she threw it towards him. He caught the ball.

When she asked him to throw it back to her, he was puzzled. He walked to her, and placed the ball on her hand, then walked back to his position to catch the ball again. Every time he walked to give the ball to her. He was not able to imitate the act of throwing the ball. He understood 'what' throwing was, but could not use his hands to do so. He began to get bored too, and walked away from the game.

Mother had to leave the game too, satisfied with her son's success in learning how to catch the ball and keeping the interest in the game for half an hour or so.

The boy was happy too, as he was able to handle the ball in the right way,

> Sphere of symmetry,
> Smooth its body,
> It rolls with grace,
> With playful happiness.

The rest of the day was passed with the 'throw and catch' way. Whatever mother found at home near her hand like potatoes, garlic, towels, bed sheets, pencil and plastic plates, became 'pretend' balls to her.

Each time she threw something, he was supposed to catch it and then encouraged to return it to her, by a throw. He went back to the sportswoman to return and waited for her to get tired. She was determined to teach and was getting impatient.

The next day she took the ball to the 'Therapy Park' of the Institute. She threw the rubber ball at the wall of the slide. The ball returned to her hand. She asked him to try. The boy eagerly did and was surprised to see that it was easy.

He had learnt how to throw the ball.

"Kaki, mother is overdoing things and I am finding no time for myself. She is bound to make me learn the things at the very moment she starts," complained the boy in the usual pointing at the letters way. He felt she was being a bit cruel as she told him "Our one day should be equal to two days."

The boy had a tendency to resist any new activity and mother was introducing too many new things at the same time. He knew that it was Kaki's words only that she would pay heed to, and the boy therefore wanted them to talk.

Kaki suggested the swimming pool for the boy. "It would help him, to get the required amount of exercise, and he would also get a trainer to interact with," she told mother.

There is no tomorrow in mother's style.

"Let's start it from today!" she happily announced, as she walked her way happily home.

The boy thought it might help. After all, he enjoyed bathing.

> The swimming pool,
> The water full,
> Looked too cool,
> The flow playful.
> But I admit,
> He was frightened a bit
> As he undressed —
> To the water he faced.
> He changed his mind
> And looked behind,
> Uncertain of his courage
> (He was below average).
> But what happened next —
> I will explain best.

The swimming pool was blue and beautiful, I admit. But the boy panicked to step down into the water. Mother was over excited and helped the boy to plunge into the pool.

"What am I supposed to do?" wondered the boy, as he watched some ladies, dressed in swimming costumes, sitting or swimming confidently.

The mermaids of the swimming pool,
My eyes are filled with you.
Wish I had a fishing net —
I could fish you out too.

   The boy was standing in knee height water and was determined to stay there. He meant it with all his heart, with all his
stiffness. Mother, ever encouraging, was giving directions to him.
   "See that boy, son, walk like him!"
   "See the little girl over there catching the rod and throwing her legs: here, catch this rod and try it."
   Our minds are strange. They judge the situations and in-
spire or discourage ourselves. (I would prefer to write patriotic
words, rather than face the war.)
   The boy was ready to watch the mermaids and appreciate their grace rather than have one of them as his trainer.
Mother was determined to make the hour useful for her son.
So she was trying to push the boy further into the water,
standing on the edge of the pool, her body bending danger-
ously in towards the water. She attracted the attention of a
mermaid, who introduced herself as the trainer:

         She came with all her grace,
         She came with her pretty face,
         She was no doubt so real,
         But the boy was a disgrace

She caught him by his arm.
With her smiling charm,
And led the boy through
The deeper waters so.
But my pretty lady,
The boy was really sorry.
Your charm would not conquer
His anxiety and his fear.
So he panicked, so he shouted,
So you left his arm afraid.
And you thought that 'let him be
To fight his fear through time — may be!'

After one hour the boy came out of the pool, with a dry body, relieved, happy and ready to go back home. Mother was tired too. "Tomorrow you won't be afraid!"

"Dear mother, why can't you understand my problems," the boy told in silence. "It is not the water I fear, but it is losing my senses in the new situation, which I fear" said the boy, within himself.

But mother was not able to understand his silence. There was no attempt to explain it that way from his side. So mother got the message that the 'water' made him afraid — like any other normal child.

The next day the boy was even more afraid. He just stood and waited for the hour to get over. He felt stiff and saw himself as a rock, very strong and heavy.

But he stood at a safe distance from where his mother could not push him like the previous day standing on the edge of the pool. She asked a girl to help him overcome his phobia, who tried to force him to sit in the shallow water. The terrified boy spray out of the pool, followed by a chase from mother, and her voice — "Get back! Get back I say!"

Swimming pool was a flop. He was relieved when mother told him that she was not taking him there any more. "Perhaps you are not yet ready for it."

The next experiment was the gymnasium. Mother was informed about it, and she introduced her son to the trainer. Although the place was an ideal place for children to develop their muscles, bones and whatever, like flexibility. Yet this very noisy environment made him deaf. He on the other hand, shouted louder to make others deaf, and rolled on the wooden floor of the basketball court, closing his eyes and escape the presence of the new situation.

His shout was so sudden that the boys left their place, and surrounded him in a ring — the so-called happy children in a world that is perfect filled with laughter and friendship!

Mother was embarrassed, and apologised for the disturbance, which was created by the sudden shout of her son. The trainer told mother that he had no problem letting the boy try, as he may react in a positive way the next time when he came. But she was needed to be with him, as they did not know how to tackle him. The arrangement thus satisfied mother. At least they did not reject him after seeing his conduct. She thanked him telling him that she would go about it, if her son was ready and willing to come. Otherwise she would not force him.

"You decide whether you should go or not. I leave it to you," she told the boy. "But no crying today."

"I am afraid to twist and turn my body," the boy pointed on the alphabet board.

"We are going there to see others twist and turn their bodies. When we get bored we can come out," mother assured him. "The only thing which I request is, try to tolerate the situation and be a better behaved boy today." She promised him that even if it were after five minutes, she would come back and not put any pressure on him.

The boy was ready to face the place, and the happy normal children. Poor mother was so tensed! To hide it, she kept on reciting the same lines, over and over again

> "Who has seen the wind?
> Neither you nor I,
> But when the trees bow down their heads,
> The wind is passing by!"

The boy was echoing it too, and felt better. They walked to the place for half an hour to stay there for five or ten minutes — as long as the boy chose.

He stayed and watched for 45 minutes. He surprised mother. He went there every evening since then and felt very good after the 'entertainment'.

But the trainer was a very busy person. He could not give individual attention to the boy.

"Why don't they call me to try with them," boy wondered, after three weeks of going and coming back. Forgetting that he was different and would be different however much he wanted to be a part of the better world, their world, his surrounding world.

> The real world of concrete
> And the sensory feel,
> It is painful to be rejected
> As with my aspirations I deal

"I will teach you how to somersault," said mother when the boy was upset. "It is not their fault. I think it is because of the shout, which they heard from you on the first day that frightened them. So they are afraid and yet finding it difficult to tell no!"

She got to work the very moment, she placed the bed mattress on the floor — she helped the boy to kneel down on it.

I must make the word 'helped' clear as my readers may frown and say "Why should a six and half years' boy need help to kneel down?"

I defend the boy, your honours, because he could not imitate, and panicked to do any new activity. Mother was aware of it, and helped him kneel, as she had done with other things, which he had learnt to do.

She bent his stiff head, practising the action over and over again. She let him take time to adjust and enjoy, then with a "ready, steady and go" she turned the legs to complete the somersault. It was fun! After a few times, he could do it independently. "I can do" he thought, satisfied himself.

"Yes, you can do everything if it is taught by someone, who is aware of your difficulties," echoed his other self, who was ambitious and full of inspiration.

Other self
'Other self' beyond my reach,
I know you are a part of me,
But when I ask you to guide my act
I am left to uncertainty.
For a situation has many ways.
This or that, may be,
'Other self' the wisdom finds,
I act with stupidity.

The next day, mother told the trainer that the boy "can somersault." If he is permitted to try with other children, he would gain confidence. The boy stood in the queue, and waited for his turn to show what he has learnt.

He was not used to standing and waiting. He felt impatient and began to flap. Mother came near him to remind that it looked bad as he was already attracting some curious looks.

When his turn came, he found that he had forgotten how to kneel and felt tensed as other boys watched. Mother was expecting this from her experience. She quickly made him do it, by helping him to kneel and then pushing him from behind. Her touch itself made him recall the act and he continued doing it (like other children) till the mark.

"Certainly we can use the place to revise what you learn!" But she had her limitations too. She could only teach him the free hand exercises and not the parallel bars, ring jumping or vaulting.

"We can wait till your speech comes when you would not need me," she suggested. It was disappointing, but she reasoned that just going and spending time there renewed her desire for a normal childhood for her son, also an easy life for herself. She also felt insecure about their lives, as there was no definite arrangement like those of the other people. She was tired and yet could afford to be tired.

* * *

They can walk on the roads as an alternate source of exercise. Enough of trying to find a trainer for him!

"Kaki, I want to know why I am not invited to your place any more?" asked the boy, thinking that she no more liked him.

"I have no objection taking you there, but you behave so badly, that others at my place wonder how effective are your therapies. You make me ashamed of your behaviour," said Kaki to him.

"How do I behave?" wondered the boy. "What is behaviour?"

His 'other self' immediately told him the definition "The way we act in a situation in projection to enable others get an impression, is behaviour."

But the word 'badly' disturbed him, as good or bad were relative terms. How could Kaki say "he behaved badly?" But it was Kaki who was giving her reason and sure it was an honourable reason!

And they have honourable reasons, considering the 'right to be unique' in the way of behaviour. People are ashamed, embarrassed or afraid of the autistics.

'Consideration' of course is the very nature of society. It gives my friends the right to judge and distinguish between 'good or bad', between normal and abnormal.

Of course, there are certainly certain considerate people who also see the grey and compromise between the normal and the distorted. They can appreciate the distorted painting of a painter as a masterpiece, with their perfectly pretty ladies accompanying them in an art display, ready to spend both on their ladies and the distorted representation of the perfect.

> You opened the door
> There was warmth
> I felt it in my heart
> I knocked it now
> For more warmth
> But turned out away, alas!

The boy was very upset when he was told that his behaviour was the reason for not being invited to her place. So he started a 'fresh ritual' of 'no evening days', as evenings were the times when he went to his Kaki's house.

I will tell what the no evening days were according to him. He tried to wipe away the presence of evenings, the time between the afternoons and dusk from his days.

He did so by switching on the light of the rooms from 3pm itself, even though sunlight entered the room. Mother tried to stop him by reasoning out that it was a foolish thing to do so. But the boy refused anything else. The 'no evening day' continued as it grew to a ritual of invitation or no invitation, there must be no evenings for him.

Mother at first used physical pressure and punishment. It

did not work. So she began her evenings with him on the roads from 3pm itself. She started her walks on the roads and bus stops, markets and parks. She showed him the sky of the evening, the colours and the architects of the colour formation — the dust particles — explaining the dispersion of sunlight.

> The brow of evening
> gold and red,
> In the wait for
> Sun to set,
> The earth at peace
> Asks for rest,
> With fading lights
> Of the west.

He began to appreciate the sunset, the earth under the evening sky, and the market slowly being lit up with bulbs. The month's evening walks were useful for the boy. He forgot about the no evening days. He waited for the evening walks.

"What makes eagerness turn to impatience?" wondered he, as one morning it made him plead to mother for the walk. She said 'no' and the boy got very upset for the rest of the day. Mother left him alone to cry.

"You should tackle it yourself" she told him, and continued with her work.

I waited for the evening
when morning was
And morning passed
with my loss.
The morning may be
not the cause,
My sorrow had
another because.

"I want to talk to Kaki," he said, after the full two hours
he spent crying. Mother was tired of the endless flow of tears,
and asked for peace, holding the alphabet board in front of
him. "I want to talk to Kaki" he pointed.

Mother rang Dr Prathibha Karanth and told her about
his fuss taking a walk. She said she was busy that day and did
not intend to let him have his way. The boy was given the
phone and Kaki spoke to him. It was a one way conversation,
as the boy had no speech. Yet it worked. He stopped crying for
the rest of the morning.

Designs and colours fascinated him for a long while. He
wanted to use the sketch pens for the designs as the inks were
brighter and were easy to use. Mother drew a sample design at
first on the top of the page. He filled the rest of the page with

four rows of the same design. He felt very relaxed as beauty and repetition made him happy.

They were simple curves and lines. Yet repeating then made them look so pretty. The boy felt proud of his designs, he went through them whenever he found time.

But there was a drawback in his drawings, as he could only copy designs but could not be creative. He did not, or in better words, 'could not' go beyond this ability, and express his imaginations through them.

He 'imagined' three-dimensional designs too, and mentally covered himself with them.

> Beyond the world of what and why
> Beyond the reasons and the concrete,
> The 'abstract' lies with a richer glory
> Somewhere in imaginations deep!

"Why to think about others?"

"What do others think of me?" the boy asked himself. He saw himself as two different selves. One was the complete one — the thinking self — which was filled with learnings and feelings. It could feel the sorrows, joys and satisfaction. It could even create the abstractness in the surroundings. But 'being in the abstract' had already faded away into the better awareness of the other self.

The other self was the acting self that behaved and had no self-control. It was weird and full of actions. The actions which this self displayed, were not symmetrical with his thoughts. His well-wishers told that it was not proper to do this or that. For example, picking food from someone else's plate was not good. Others would think that the boy had been told nothing about manners, specially when he was growing up. I must specify this point. He would pick up any object that attracted his physical self, through its colour, smell and appearance.

Once a table fan had attracted him and he went to touch it. He cut his fingers, of course, but could not caution himself, though he had full knowledge of current, electricity and the dangers involved with it.

The two selves stayed in their own selves, isolated from each other.

Picking up objects often made mother very embarrassed specially when the object was food. She was worried as whenever she asked the boy to explain his act on the alphabet board, the boy said that his wisdom gets defeated to his greed and he picks up the food, forgetting everything.

So they decided to eat outside once a week, every Saturday.

She would also have a good time, as she really did not like the 'everyday' cooking.

She chose a 'neat' restaurant for the Saturdays. As she placed the order, she made sure that the boy had a proper posture. She started to converse with him as the boy might get impatient, and show some awkward gestures, causing unwanted attention.

It was very difficult to wait, but the constant assurance from her was very useful that he was behaving like a 'perfect gentleman' and he was making her proud.

The boy got used to eating out with other people eating near him. He looked forward to the Saturdays, as it became their marketing days also.

He no more picked up objects from the shops or the tomatoes from the vegetable vendors. He learnt to wait as his mother bought the things and learnt not to walk away from her, as getting lost could be dangerous.

Practice and assurance was needed for his market and crowd tolerance.

When the earth is wet with dew
And morning is fresh and new.
The eastern glow
Rising steady, yet slow
Told "Happy birthday to you!"

The boy turned seven and was very disappointed to see that he had high fever. He expected his father to be surprised.

His father was not aware of the fact that his son has started to talk, as the boy and his mother had planned to keep it a secret and would surprise him when he would visit them. The boy was expecting a celebration but he woke up with a high fever and a bitter taste inside his mouth.

There needs a flash back to show how the 'talking' started.

The month of May was it
Kaki's father was very sick
She was very anxious too.
As his end time drew,
The boy had seen a death
And the tears that it left.
So he decided to try
And cheer Kaki's tears dry.

"How happy your speech would make her when she comes back after the funeral" encouraged mother.

It was the 26th of May 1995. Kaki had left Mysore to attend her father's funeral and was not to be back for at least a week.

"If not now, then never" the boy thought. "If not today, then never" his other self agreed. For the first time, his two selves were communicating. The 'voice' was but yet to co-operate.

The problem of autism was making him feel that his

voice was a distant substance that was required to be collected and put somewhere inside his throat. But he was unable to find it. He wept for it.

When mother asked him about the cause, he replied that he was weeping for the death.

"But don't you think that it is rather unusual to go to that extent when you were not familiar with the person who has passed away" argued mother, "I think you can do a more constructive thing by writing it down in your note book." So for a while the boy forgot about his voice and adjusting it to the right position in his throat.

> He wrote about death
> In the hope to escape
> Let the problem be kept
> Be buried by the death.
> But the writing got over when
> His problem worried him again.

"Mother I can't find my voice," said the boy, very desperate, as his other self was reminding him "If not today, then never!"

The idea came to mother like a battery charged in a torch. She told him to relax and asked him to sit with a loose body.

Then she did 'it' with all her suddenness. She gave him a

push from the back on his chest. The boy was not prepared for the push, and he gave a sound "uh!" as air pushed out of his mouth due to the reflex action of the push.

"There! Your voice is found! Now with each push, you will find it," she told him. Then for the next 10 minutes, they did the voice finding process.

She then kept a glass of water in front to him. "Now with every push I give you, find your voice and ask me to give to you water."

She gave the boy the first push, and the boy said "uh!" meaning 'I'. At the second push he said "wah", the first part of the word 'want'. Then with the third push, he said "tuh", the later part of the word 'want'. Similarly with the next two pushes, he said "wuh" and "tuh" for the word 'water'. Mother gave him the water, asking him what he wanted to do with it. Then she gave him a push and the boy said "druh", the first part of the word 'drink', then with the next push, he said 'th' replacing the 'k' sound with 'th!' Mother was not very keen on the pronunciation. She was glad that the way was found to get some verbal output from him.

"Why didn't we try it before?" she regretted, after the boy answered her question. "What is two times five?" and pushed him.

The boy replied "tuh" for 'ten'.

That evening the boy spent time by replying to mother's

questions which were usually needing a one word answer. The method was the same — the push and speak way.

He said "sah" and "vah" for the number 7 when she asked him what would three and four be? There were two pushes needed.

Then before going to the toilet, the boy was asked to state it. With each push he said "uh", "wah", "tah", "gah", "tuh", "tuh", "tuh", for the statement 'I want to go to toilet'. Of course, my dear readers can count the number of pushes that was required for a simple sentence like that.

In the next two days, the boy got used to her questions as they did some picture reading ranging between 'what' and 'who'. But she yet did not ask the 'why' questions because she did not want the speech to bore him with 'double promotion and triple promotion of long sentences.'

I shall tell you a secret, dear readers. She was afraid lest her son stops his 'acquired' speech and again gets de-motivated before Dr Prathibha Karanth was back from her father's funeral. So she kept on reminding him what a remarkable achievement he had made and how surprised she would be as she was his main motivator.

It was very noble of her not to reveal this achievement to anybody else except his then speech therapist Aish Kant Rout, who began the same picture reading method. He was trying to add the words "This is a . . ." to the questions. "What is this?" which the boy felt rather tiring and a 'baby like approach'.

There is no fun in answering, if freedom is restricted to the rules of a disciplined sentence.

Kaki came back after some days and the first thing which mother did was to call her from the local telephone office to give her the message about the boy's speech. She also told her that she is letting him say the words the way he is choosing to say. So his speech had a lot of distortions.

But she did not mention about the 'push and tell' way to her on the phone.

(I will now discuss about the 'push and find the voice' way, how it helped the boy and sometimes still helps him to answer a new voice.)

Previously, it was just a reminder as switch on your voice and answer. At first the answers were one worded and did not require much care and freedom. The person questioning knew the answer to the 'what is this?' or 'who is this?'

But growth is the rule of any beginning. Slowly the 'how?' and 'why' were begun by mother. One push and some nods were needed to time the answer. Then mother or Aish Kant had to repeat the words which the boy told in the end as a substitute for the push. Then he proceeded to the next word.

Pushing also helped him to be attentive, as he sometimes

stopped half way, keeping the statement incomplete. Pushing helped in the production of a louder sound as air comes out of the mouth with the sound.

In the later stage, pushing may be replaced by a press in any part of the body.

(But I feel that it was something which does not look very 'natural', and so it is better to outgrow the habit. But it should be a gradual replacement and not a sudden imposition. As for the autistics, any sudden change creates a kind of help-lessness, which de-motivates them.)

But there definitely needs to be a change as every begin-ning has to proceed.

I would tell the people, those who deal with the autistics, "Try follow the same system, which works best for your subject consistently and universally. At that time, there should not be any 'social customs' that comes in the way of the pro-cedure. It may look very 'unnatural' when a person is pushed or urged to speak, but it would be a great help for your subject."

I shall also suggest that non-verbal autistics need more stimulation than the verbal autistics, the use of a 'mild touch' is less effective than a sudden push or tap.

No, dear psychologists, you do not make yourselves in-human by the hurt, which may cause a slight pain. You would make the person aware of his body through the pain, helping him to function.

Wish my legs had the wings of a bird
And fly me to afar.
I would gather the raindrops from every cloud
To wash my every tear.
Then I would take the blue of the sky,
With the gold of the sun.
And light my world with the hope of day
Then see my dreams return.

His seventh birthday was a flop as he was in bed for the whole day due to fever. His father reached Mysore only late at night. He was not able to hear the boy speak as he was fast asleep by the time he reached home.

The next day he heard his son speak, but did not show much surprise. The boy was very depressed. He had expected a greater astonishment in his father's face.

I now realise that he had probably failed to understand his son's speech and did not find the push and talk method very impressive.

But he did take them out to compensate for the loss of his birthday. He said that the boy can have a whole birth week. Celebration for the birthday cause was not what the boy had sought, with the 'finding of his voice'.

That relief to him had brought,
For many a day he had fought

And faced difficulties a lot.
The road to this birthday was not smooth,
His eagerness was thus cooled.
Hence he flew in the bird like way.
To find the blue and gold sun rays.

The problem of taking down dictation was also dealt by the therapist called Mrinal.

The boy could not write any letter or number, if he was asked to write, without the presence of the board.

Suppose the required letter was A, the picture of A did not form immediately in his mind. This does not mean he could not recognise A, from a jumbled group of alphabets.

The boy was also upset when he had found out this problem with himself.

Practice, practice, more practice and the nothing less was the solution. Pages of his notebook were filled up with alphabets till the satisfying improvement was reached.

The numbers were also learnt to 'recall and write' in the same way. One thing should follow the other, and so the dictation of spelling also started with similar sounding words first. For example, 'and', 'band', 'hand' and so on, the usual way they teach the spelling.

The difference here was that the boy was not learning the spelling, but learning to represent them on a paper.

The fragmented world needed unification.
Fragmented world of fear and pieces,
Beyond 'our' understanding and reaches,
Broken into bits and parts,
With the cause of our escaping hearts!

This song is not sung lightly by the autistic hearts. This is a reason for their withdrawal. This is the reason for their escape.

How do I say it with such surerity? I say it from my own experience, as each stage I passed, sensing the taste of improvement with my personal development, to a stage when I got the motivation to write this story.

My story, through the boy of the story.

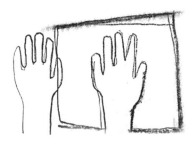

Epilogue

Today, the fragmented self of hand and body parts which I once saw myself as, have unified to a living 'me', striving for a complete 'me'. Not in the abstract existence of the impossible world of dreams but a hope for a concrete dream of this book to reach those who would like to understand us through me.

If this book is able to light even one little flame, I would be able to see my dream take its shape.

No, I still am not perfect and need the social co-operation for my growth.

It pains when people avoid us and the schools refuse to take us. I faced it and felt that every day there may be others like me who are facing the social rejection like me. I must make the point clear that it is not lack of social understanding which causes the weird behaviour, but it is lack of getting to use oneself in the socially acceptable way, which causes the weird or the undesirable behaviour.

The expressing ability also varies in the situations which divert from the norm. There was a limitation with me, when I laughed or screamed at pleasant feelings, flapped or cried when situations got difficult to cope with.

Situations are unique in their own ways, and causes the insecurity in the hearts of the autistics, leading to fear, causing intolerance to a new setting of surroundings.

The exposure to variations, be it clothes or food, place or timetable, help us to, if not love, but to tolerate and understand our role in the situations better.

We cannot have a voice modulation as it requires a lot of voice control which may need some super effort. So we say things in a flat tone with seldom use of commas and questions, though I congratulate myself in 'finding my voice'.

I congratulate myself for every milestone which I overcame, as I fought with my own resistance.

One day I dream that we can grow in a matured society where nobody would be 'normal or abnormal' but just human beings, accepting any other human being — ready to grow together.

A world of such
Can't it be?
With acceptance and love
Not sympathy!
My story could touch
If your heart,
My 'hope' would get
The precious reward!

Beyond the silence

In Somewhere

And let past be buried in its own heaviness as I allow my life to go ahead with time, as I know that it is time alone which will help me move ahead with my biological age.

And I wonder and still I wonder what have the little boy in the past two years achieved after having found himself not as the fragmented body parts, but as a complete self, determined to reach that total completeness which his biological age would let him achieve.

And I wonder and still wonder how to find out what the boy has achieved in the two years which have the memories of some laughter, some disappointment, some hopes and most important of all, some satisfaction.

Yet satisfaction is as momentary as the time and it leads me to keep myself wondering whether or not I am really satisfied. The more I wonder, I get lost in that absolute maze which leads me to every corner of nowhere.

The boy has definitely reached somewhere and I try to come back from that helpless nowhere. Yet the trouble with somewhere is that it is finite. It can be defined and also measured. It cannot be open ended like the infinite nowhere. When you travel through nowhere, and stop at some infinite randomness, you are still at nowhere. This cannot be possible when you are limited to the limit of somewhere. So the boy of my story in the past two years has a finite position watching the hands of the clock move and the pages of the calendar turn.

Still the buried past comes as a ghost of the painful memories to mock the present moment. It is then that somewhere meets nowhere and I lose my much coveted satisfaction making this satisfaction a momentary affair.

And yet living in the past adds to the burden of disparity. So I have to continue my Voice of Silence with my own voice and try my best to bury the past into a self dug grave, so that I can analyse my own self into the exactness of my stand in that place called 'somewhere'.

Search for a House

1996 February it was. Just like any other day. The sun was not extra bright and not extra dull. Neither was the day extra something compared to any other day. Yet it was an important day in my life because it was a definite turning point of my life. I had to choose between the security of a known circumstance of the every day speech therapy or the uncertainty of the new situation which I would face.

Dr Prathibha Karanth who has been my guide all through my 'nowhere' days announced her voluntary retirement from the All India Institute of Speech and Hearing.

I panicked within while I saw my mother fret as she discussed me and what to be done next, with her. A thousand 'ifs' and 'then what's' gathered from every where to crowd my mind as my body turned into a mere breathing matter. I was frightened of being uprooted. And then I was more or less used to a certain way of life in Mysore. It would be difficult to give it up completely. I felt the pain of giving up the bond which I had developed with the Institute.

But then the bond which I had felt with Dr Karanth was stronger.

I made up my mind. I will move over to Bangalore where she will be.

> And movements are better than stagnation
> And thus I welcomed my new destination
> And then I tried to calm my mind
> As every past should be left behind.

"I shall not leave immediately. . . ."

"Till then there is time. You can start looking for a place to stay. . . ."

"Let me come back from Brazil first. . . ."

Conversations between her and mother interrupted my thoughts as I saw my mother getting excited over the whole issue. And I knew very well that she works best when she gets that look on her face.

She did not wait. The very next day we were off to Bangalore by the first train. Before we got down she had told at least a dozen passengers why we were heading for Bangalore. All of them had given her their contact numbers and promised to help. She took them down religiously while I knew that she will do it alone.

We bought a map of Bangalore and sat on a vacant bench to decide where to start. The map had drawn a lot of attention and soon I found three pairs of interested eyes looking at the map. She folded the map back and walked away with me to the city of Bangalore. The city of promises beckoned me.

Cobweb of Uncertainty

Soon a monthly ticket from Mysore to Bangalore was purchased as mother realised that finding a house was not a 'one day affair'.

Dr Prathibha Karanth had already shifted to Bangalore and saw me twice a week at the Institute of Speech and Hearing with the same affection while I discovered that 'home is truly where the heart is'.

It was a month of great excitement. Getting up before any crow got up, getting dressed after a brisk bath and off on the road to catch the first bus which took us dutifully to the railway station each day through the lamp lit streets on mist filled mornings.

I had begun to love this uncertainty as I found that I had ample scope to guess what 'cans' and 'cannots' awaited us.

I tried to guess what sort of people would accompany us through the three hour long journey. Will the Bald and the Bearded man who was curiously looking at me while I was flapping my hands the previous day come along?

This phyla for uncertainty developed since then. It was a completely different feeling from my early days, when I preferred the same clothes, same routes, and lost myself in new situations. I was determined to make use of this newfound desire to guess the unknown.

'What is that man sitting on that corner seat thinking?'

'Why is that man whose legs are so fat looking at his watch so often? Why is he so impatient? Will he get a shout from his Boss if he is late? Will he blame the train?'

Thoughts of speculations and thoughts of doubts covered the mind into a new kind of cobweb and I occasionally flapped them away, while mother tried her best to show me a distant tree through the window.

The cobweb of uncertainty remained. Mother kept a heavy bag on my hand to prevent me from further flapping. I saw cobwebs forming around the bag, spreading through the bag, infecting the whole compartment, and then engulfing the train reaching further and further beyonds.

The world was covered with a cobweb of uncertainty.

Home

"Your son is not normal. We cannot allow you to stay in our house." The land lady told with a lot of firmness and meant it.

Mother and I had shifted to Bangalore just two days back. Bangalore was a new place for us, and the house was within our budget.

Moreover, we had found the house after a long search by doing up and down trip from Mysore to Bangalore every day. Yes, it was difficult to do it all over again with no one to help.

"He will not disturb anyone," mother had tried to explain.

I felt hurt too and tried to point on my board of communication that I would not disturb any one. It was not believed.

In those days, when I had found my voice, I needed the facilitation of touch to speak. My speech was also not clear and many people wondered whether I ever spoke or was my mother making it all up. So with strangers, I rarely tried to use my voice. Now, when the lady ignored my board communication, I was naturally very hurt and frustrated. I flapped my hands with despair.

"See, he is not normal because I haven't seen any normal child doing that. More or less, I have made up my mind. You must go."

Mother started it all over again. She was out on the roads and she was in the offices of the real estate agents, following them as they took her around. The cobweb of uncertainty covered all over I went while I tried to see my speculations through the mesh.

Finally a house was found and I could see a large heart welcoming us.

Home is where the heart is. My father who works in Bihar came down to be by our side while the repacking and reshifting to the big hearted house took place.

The cobweb of uncertainty disappeared.

School called Anvesh

The city of Bangalore has a strange combination. On one hand it is too traditional while on the other hand it is more modern than many other place I have seen. I had to classify myself to fit somewhere in this city.

I had to establish myself in my own way. But before getting established, I had to get acceptance. The first place of getting acceptance was a school.

When Dr Karanth took me and my mother to one such school. I read the board. It said 'Anvesh'. It was rather a strange name for any school.

The children were doing some drama rehearsal. I was more interested in the well which lay at a corner. I peeped in. My reflection peeped out. The circular parapet caused a circular sky to reflect out along with my head at that further end. I waved my hands and greeted my shadow deep down there.

I forgot that I was in a school. I forgot that the school had a strange name. I forgot that there were curious eyes around me and I forgot that the Principal was a bit hesitant to accept me.

I was asked to come there the next day for half a day. I spent the next day peeping into the well while the boys sat in the classes.

"Come my little bird, let us go to the class," the Principal called me with an invitation. I did not move. I am not sure why I did not move. But I can remember that I was so used to certain voices which I heard often like mother's and Dr Karanth's that I could not respond to any other voice. I was expecting her to lead me to the class. She was not aware of my expectations. The gap remained and I had to lose my chance of acceptance.

I was a misfit and I had to give up visiting the well. I definitely would miss my peeping shadow.

Ding dong bell
Shadow in the well.

A Wedding

"I do not want to attend the wedding mother," I had tried to explain my discomfort to mother. I had to face a big crowd of relatives of a totally different wavelength. I had already a reputation of being an awkward human specie in the family and the thought of facing all of them made me all the more nervous. I was apprehensive about the whole matter.

"I am helpless too," mother tried to explain. "He is my only brother and he will be hurt if I don't go."

"You have to choose between your son and your brother," I had threatened.

"I choose the years for my son but three days for my brother," she stopped me.

My uncle who was getting married had welcomed me more warmly than I had expected. He took me around the town on his motor cycle and soon we started to interact on the level which was common to both of us. Things were going pretty well until the day before the wedding when relatives started coming in.

All of them tried to show their total concern for mother's life.

"My God! What have you done to your health. You should take care of yourself also as you take care of your son."

Mother was uncomfortable too. She pulled me aside and told me not to be bothered much about it.

"How can it be possible mother. Take me somewhere else and teach me."

I will explain this statement. I felt the need to keep myself occupied all the time and did not know what to do with myself when I had no work to do. I was feeling lost without any activity.

'How can I teach you in this crowd? You take some magazines and look at them.' The solution was simple but the act was not that simple for me. I ran around the place to show my helplessness.

> All the world was a busy place
> And I was an idle kind
> Disqualified in the human race
> A different form of mind.

My father tried to physically pull me back, like they pull a chained dog back. In that confusion a family well wisher tried to practice palmistry by reading my palm. What he said did not matter any more. Nothing mattered any more. I was labelled 'sick'. Mentally sick.

So what if I wrote better than most? So what if I wrote poems?

The world was a suitable place for the social beings and not beings like us. Mother was also a social being!

My longest 'three days' ended.

Shanti

"Why don't you meet Ms Shanti," the gentleman suggested mother. "She is the Principal of the Marathoma Opportunity School."

Mother was desperate to find a school for me. I was desperate to be accepted by anybody. Anywhere.

"So be it," said mother. We went to the Marathoma Opportunity School. The children were all outside doing some exercises. They were completely organized group. I had learnt how to do the exercises when I was in Mysore. It is making your body parts move as someone said "ONE, TWO, THREE, FOUR . . ." etc. It is easier than any game because it is predictable. You can predict that one will be followed by two and two will be followed by three. You can know before hand what to do when number one or number two is called out.

"I would love to do it," I told mother. In fact, I was ready to do anything which would make me be accepted.

I went inside Ms Shanti's office. She did not look with any hesitation at me. I was thankful. I want to clarify this point. I had no eye contact with any one. But I could understand the glances from the other body languages which the person carried. I have read facts that autistics fail to understand body languages. Personally I am more sensitive to the attitudes of the people. When I know that someone is watching me with curiosity, I feel uneasy. My body reacts to it immediately. I become hyperactive and flap my hands to release some of my stress.

Ms Shanti did not hesitate to look at me. So I was thankful. She asked me to sit. Once again I was thankful.

Mother was direct. "Will you admit my son? He is autistic."

"What is your name?" Ms Shanti asked me. I was thankful because she was not talking about me, but to me. Soon I was conversing with her through my communication board.

> Lady so calm like the whispering night
> Lead me on into your light
> And I seek that calm in your words
> Thank you for your words and trust.

"I think you should meet Ms Veronica Mathias. She is the right person to help you." Shanti told us.

Whispering Lady

> Was it a Monday
> Or a Tuesday
> May be a Wednesday, I care not
> For that morning
> With bright sun shining
> Will forever be fresh in my thoughts.

The gate was open as if it welcomed us, mother and me. Mother, who never walks slowly hesitated to enter. She slowed down. I took the lead and she followed. I have a special instinct which allows me to know where I shall be welcomed. Till now, I have never went wrong.

I inspected the brass handle on the wooden door while mother took a deep breath of hesitation and rang the bell. The lady of the house opened the door. The face of the lady was still unknown to me, as I never looked at anyone's face. But her voice was soft to my ears, almost like a whisper.

> Whisper of hope in my ears
> Why do they echo yet so clear?
> If I told that, with sincere
> Would you still hold me dear?

The house was a world of books. Here a book, there a book, every where a book! I pulled a book from here and then a book from there. There were eight chairs and sofas to sit on. I chose to sit on this chair then changed my mind and chose to sit on that sofa. I tried to try out anything and felt like a free bird.

Mother followed me to discipline me by pulling my hands and nudging me with an elbow prick. The lady did not mind. As long as she did not mind, I could be a free bird.

I would like to explain this point clearly. When I was in

a spacious surrounding, with unlimited options, I always felt it rather difficult to choose. Choosing where to be, choosing what to do and choosing how to position myself. As a result, I got hyperactive in such a place. It can be similar to an air molecule which moves with more randomness in an open area. I felt overwhelmed with the whole situation. Too many good things. Books, chairs, windows, whispering lady and my favourite green colour on the walls.

And thank God, the lady saw my poetry; and thank God, she read some of them; and thank God she believed me! Then there were greater thanks to God for our coming days as we came closer to be friends and later something more than a friend.

> Now I look at your eyes
> And regret my age and my size
> It is true o' Veronica Mathias.

Two Days Wait

"Can I have a few copies of his poetry?" Lady Mathias asked mother.

My poetry felt honoured. It was as if they were written for that moment. I needed to write more for such moments. And I needed more of 'such moments' to keep myself on the move.

"When are we going to visit the Lady, mother?" I had asked her.

"Wednesday," said mother. "Then, if we still cannot find a school for you, we will plan to go back to Bihar." Mother had tried to put the words with such a calm voice as though nothing was wrong. I knew that she was worried. Terribly worried. She still could not rely on Lady Mathias and it was still Monday.

There were two more days to go before Wednesday. She took me out on Monday, again on Tuesday and aimlessly walked through the streets and roads. Any street and any road. I did not disturb her, as I knew that she needed it out that way.

I was in fact enjoying the markets with the noise and the colours.

Streets so full on a market place,
Traffic always on the race,
The Holy cow with all her grace
Sits and watches in solace
Tomatoes, onions and cabbages,
Colour the footpaths with greens and reds
All the market on all days
Looks with cheer of youthfulness.

Wednesday morning had arrived and I was told by mother not to hope for the sky, Acceptance, was like the sky for me. Only time could tell whether I could reach it or not. Yet I knew that 'the Whispering Lady' would help me.

> And in my secret mind I was
> Hoping to meet her, for any cause,
> Of course time has moved ahead,
> After that long 'two days' wait.

Finding a School

Lady Mathias took us around several schools which provide special education to children. Yes, I could impress all of the authorities. Finally, we came to the Spastic Society of Karnataka.

Big gate led to a big heart and in the big heart of the school were children with some or the other 'have nots'. I could at once identify with them.

The Principal Mrs Krishnaswami was seated behind the table of a cosy room, which was her office also. She was introduced to me by Lady Mathias. I felt very comfortable to communicate with her. I knew I would be accepted.

Lady Mathias had brought me to the right person. A person who was not curious about me but who respected me like an individual.

The memories stand out so clear
Of the first day in the 'School of cheer'
For my days that were yet to be
In the campus of Spastic Society.

My Handwriting

Purnima Rao was to be in charge of me.

Where to start and how to start was her problem.

I was only too happy to be accepted by the school.

There was the swing, there was the jungle jim and plenty of space to play and be a free bird.

But a school was a school.

And the school had to be with some rules.

I was as undisciplined as ever. Being a free bird was not expected from any student. I got addicted to the swing, with the breeze which I felt on my face along with the to and fro movements.

"Catch me if you can!" Ms Purnima tried to call me affectionately at first. The 'free bird' did not heed. Slowly there began sharper and sharper calls until I got down from the swing. At this point I must refer that I needed to be facilitated to do any new work at a new voice's command.

Soon Ms Purnima could communicate with me. She was consistent and that helped me not only to sit better in a working environment, but also improve my writing.

About my hand writing, I should say that people wondered whether it should be read from left to right, or from right to left. And believe me, I was shamelessly proud of it.

For days and through weeks, she worked with me to bring my angular writing to form curves. Each time I went back to my original patterns, she rubbed it out and I had to rewrite. Frustrating, but effective.

Mother followed up at home because the consistency needed to be maintained.

About Ms Purnima,

> And in rare but determined way
> She worked the mornings of her day
> I wish I had found her softer side
> That she forced and kept in hide.

My First Day in a Class Room

My first experience in a class room was rather a very confusing affair. I had never seen any classroom. My knowledge of the classroom was limited to the stories which were written about schools and from the stories which my mother told me about her school days.

The class room of the Spastic Society did not have that Spartan look. The uniformity of the sitting arrangement was not there. The first look at it told me that I could be a free bird here too.

In fact, it was a totally different situation for me and I did not know my exact role in it. So I went across the room, over looking the teacher, and over looking and ignoring the students, as if no one existed. I reached for the books kept on the book shelf.

Ms Geetha Shankar was to be my class teacher. She invited me to my seat. I remember my reluctance to sit. In fact, my body was not yet ready for it. I needed more practice to sit in a situation like that. It is still difficult, as I fight my own resistance day and again.

Ms Geetha Shankar was taking a chapter on subtraction of a bigger number from a smaller one which gave a negative answer.

I could keep my interest going for 15 minutes. I had learnt it years back from mother. I got up to walk around the room, and be a free bird once more. Mother was needed to sit with me for at least sometime till I understood the concept that being a free bird was not expected from me at least in a class room.

"How was the class?" mother asked.

"Puzzling," I replied. "I think the wheel chairs were interesting. Wish I could sit on one."

Handling the Computer

"Dare you touch it," she warned me again as I fidgeted with the mouse. Purnima Rao was seated next to me and the computer was in front of us. I had refused to look at it and even declared a total non cooperation with her. It happens to most of the autistic people like me. Any new activity is resisted by the body system.

When two stubborn heads meet, there is no compromising way! We sat there. She, looking at me, and I, looking at a mark on the wall, trying to imagine that it was an eye of the wall, or perhaps the nose, or perhaps anything else.

Purnima Rao was trying to repeat it again.

Then something interesting happened. I saw my reflection on the screen of the monitor. 'Why did I miss it before?' I wondered. I agreed to look at it on my conditions. I would look at it, provided I saw my reflection on it! When she switched it on, the light on the screen wiped it off. So I switched it off again.

"Dare you switch it off!" She had warned.

But now I had found a different interest. I pressed a key, and rows of a letter got typed. 'Nice game' I decided. Head of stubbornness met its match once more.

I finally compromised, when I was promised 10 minutes on the swing.

And the days seem long past gone
In some yonder past
Yet they are fresh, to stay with me
Forever in my heart.

Mrs Vijaya Prema

Mrs Krishnaswami felt the need for me to decentralise my studies from mother as the only teacher, to others as the teachers. Mrs Vijaya Prema was to take a special class for me where she would tell me stories and also interact with me.

It happens to me that I am very sensitive to voices. Any new voice is frightening to me and it takes time for me to adjust to it. Usually people get frustrated and give up. However, if the person is persistent and maintains the same pitch, I can slowly get used to the voice.

Mrs Vijaya Prema was persistent. She came every day with a planned time table. She began the class with an activity like a game. The game varied from a jig saw puzzle to a memory game. Sometimes she brought crayons and papers to colour.

I, by my ability and by my autism am not a very expressive person when it comes to drawing and colouring. I tend to draw the same car or the same tree or a same rectangle when pencil and papers are given to me, without meaning anything. I cannot represent my thoughts on paper as a diagram.

So when Mrs Vijaya Prema tried to give me colours I tried to fill the page with rectangles with any random colour which I happened to pick up.

I however got used to her presence and then to her voice. She read out a story from a text book. I always dislike the dull text book stories because they are filled with all those 'shoulds and should nots'.

But I enjoyed being with her although I did not appreciate the stories which she read out to me. I began to communicate with her through the communication board.

The aim was achieved. I could communicate with one more person.

Using the Racquet

"Now hold the racquet where I am holding." Mother facilitated me. She would teach me tennis or badminton or in simple words, how to hit the ball or anything with a bat.

I needed time to understand what she wanted me to do at first, and it being difficult for me, as it was a new activity, I was very passive. It needed a lot of concentration and positioning of the body. The feel of the racquet in my hand, made a kind of imbalance in my body. I had to get adjusted to my heavy right hand with which I was holding the racquet, and certainly tended to loosen my grip from it, letting it fall, which mother was constantly picking up for me. I was also walking all around, as I could not stand in one place during those days other than holding on to something.

Mother kept her hold on my shoulder with one hand, while with the other hand, she held the racquet with me. Whenever I tried to loosen my grip off it, she made me hold it back. Then she made me hit the ball on the wall. When the ball returned back, she made me hit it again, and then again.

At first it was she who was using all her force to hit the ball. Slowly I began to understand it. She loosened her grip from my hand and my shoulders slowly, as I began to gain confidence.

There was only one racquet. So she brought my hard bound note book which would be her proxy racquet for the time being. She stood by the wall where I was hitting the ball. Since I did not have any control over my hands, the ball was going any where and every where. Mother proved to be an excellent athlete. She ran here and she ran there to challenge the any where's and every where's, while I tried to concentrate on the ball.

Then I hit the ball so hard, that it got lost.

"No problem," said mother. She tore a page from my note book and made a ball shape by crumpling it.

The first lesson on tennis or badminton or whatever got over.

Obeying Self Commands

How to conduct my self when the body is constantly trying to find some stability? By this I mean to say that some times I felt that my body was made of just my head while sometimes I felt that it was made of just my legs. It was very difficult to feel the complete body when I was not doing anything.

Sometimes I had to knock my head or slap it to feel it. Of course from my knowledge of biology I knew that I had voluntary muscles and involuntary muscles. I also knew that my hands and legs were made of voluntary muscles. But I experimented with myself that when I ordered my hand to pick up a pencil I could not do it. I remember long back when I had ordered my lips to move I could not do it.

When I asked my mother about it, she said that she did not have an answer to it. But she said that the next month will have 'that' target which we will both work for. She also told me not to feel different and get worried with it.

"Now give a command to yourself. I will facilitate you."

When she facilitated me things were simple, as her touch made me feel that part of my body with which I was to perform that task.

"I will pick up my pencil," I had told myself.

She put five objects in front of me. She touched my shoulders and I picked the pencil.

"Now keep the verb 'pick' common and order yourself to pick any of these five objects," she told me.

I had learnt to order myself, the verb pick and follow that command.

The next verb was 'keep' and then 'throw' and so on. In my coming days, the Sensory Integration Program, helped me to develop it further.

Sensory Integration Program

Sensory Integration Program. By this I mean to say, it helps all the senses to work together.

I had a definite problem. When I concentrated on the sound, I felt my eyes and nose shutting off. I could never do everything together at the same time. That is, I could not see you and at the same time hear you. My sense of hearing was always sharper than my sight. This is the reason, I never used my eyes to interact with anybody. Psychologists call it 'lack of eye contact'.

The result was the knowledge of a fragmented world perceived through isolated sense organs. It is because of my learning of books, that I could tell that the environment was made of the trees and air, living and non living, this and that.

I could use the words and learned language better because of my hearing ability with a vague idea what the words looked like or felt like.

Ms Shubhangi Dhuru is an occupational therapist who tirelessly helped me to overcome it to some extent. The therapy takes up some activities and exercises which enables one to be aware of one's body as well as the position of the body in space. There are hanging, climbing, bouncing, rolling and jumping activities to begin with which makes you aware of your body better.

Once you are aware of your body, you enjoy it. Once you enjoy it, you appreciate it. Once you appreciate it, you perform better. You for instance want to look good with a yellow shirt rather than a white. I have also planned a moustache for me when I come of age.

Any way, all my abilities go back to my book knowledge of Biology which mother had taught me and because of which I enjoyed my every transformation.

Otherwise, I could not have appreciated my improvement the way I have.

Learning How to Read

Ms Raksha works with me as a speech therapist ever since I am in Bangalore. It was she who motivated me to read. All my learning was restricted through hearing, understanding and then remembering.

Mother's voice was my main source of learning. Mother

had to read out every thing from text books to story books because I could not keep my eyes on any page for a long time.

However we need to improve our performances and cannot stay where we are.

Ms Raksha helped me to learn how to read. I have mentioned earlier how facilitation works with my body system. Unknowingly Ms Raksha was facilitating me when she started to read with me in chorus, with the intention to improve my speech, which Dr Karanth had suggested her to do.

When she read, I had to naturally follow the words in order to keep pace with her speed. Slowly my concentration improved and I could keep my eyes fixed on a page without getting distracted.

Mother practised it at home and within a month I read a two hundred page book, reading about seven pages a day, reading in chorus with mother.

Today I can read my own books without facilitation. But I still feel good if someone reads with me as a motivating factor.

Ms Raksha has helped me to read without the least idea of what a great a self confidence I have gained through it.

My Stand Today

Today I stand in a better position compared to what it was two years back but I definitely need further self improvement.

I still need mother or my class teacher Ms Geetha Shankar to sit by my side not as facilitators, but as my environment which helps me to retain the flow with my language and communication. I am certain that with more socialisation I will generalise this.

It is still difficult to follow a stranger's voice specially when he expects answers. I get worked up. Usually mother repeats the question and then I understand it, as I am conditioned to her voice.

I can speak although many people cannot follow because it is not clear. Sometimes I need facilitation to begin my speech like opening a speech door in my throat. To facilitate me mother has to wave her hands. I suppose I will not need it in a year or so.

I still flap my hands when I am deep in my thoughts. But I stop when I am told about it. I am not able to check myself when I see my favourite food and cause a great embarrassment to mother. Had I known what embarrassment felt like I could improve myself, although I know it is a letting down feeling.

Yet with all my haves and have knots I remain a total optimistic person because I have many well wishers who constantly encourage me to achieve my dreams.

So I am able to continue my dreams not as the stair case climbing dream which I once did and which led me to nowhere, but I dream of being an independent person one day capable of living my own life.

And dreams begin and dreams end
Yet in dreams I depend
Dreams of truth and dreams of vain
Dreams of joy and dreams of pain.

Epilogue

Nothing is more frustrating than an incomplete story. And nothing is more frustrating for a story teller if he does not know how to complete his story, specially when the story is about himself.

There can be any ending to it. The absolute ending will be revealed to him only at the moment of his last breath. He will be so filled with his own thoughts, at that moment, that he may not be able to write about that absolute time of his life. So his story will never be completed to tell others how it ended.

When I had written Voice of Silence, at the age of eight, little did I realise that I will have something to add to it. It had looked as a complete book in itself.

Yet life continued and taught me that my story will continue till the moment of my last breath and may be beyond it also. May be it was there before my first breath had taken place. For I have realised that every effect has a cause. So there must be a cause to my imperfection. If I asked you "Why on earth do I live as an autistic person and you as a normal person," what will you answer?

All men are not equal in the eyes of God, as the great preachers have claimed. So be it. And His will is always done. And it is again upon His will how my story will end. Only there can be guesses and speculations built on the platform of my hopes and dreams, which have no place in this book.

> And hopes and dreams which mind has seen
> Beyond the reach of life
> Yet those dreams fill the thoughts
> Yet they grow and thrive.

All Through the
Rainbow Path

This book is born out of a realization of a lonely world which the mentally challenged person faces. The characters are totally imaginary and bear no resemblance to anybody I know of.

Yet when time stares at face
Yet when life seems meaningless
Ask yourself all your bless
For some like you may have less.

I

Heavens

The cloud was once again forming a mist around my eyes as I tried to gaze up at the sky, where I suppose the heavens should be.

They say that the heavens are in the upward direction and so must it be, as they are never wrong. They say so many things and they say with their knowledge of them. Sure they are never wrong. I hear all that they say. Their words cover my eyes like this cloud which has covered it since morning. I wait.

I can wait as long as the light of the day is suspended around me. I wait for the clouds to go and clear the sky I can see the heavens. And one day perhaps I would find the God there. But as usual I know that nothing will happen. The sky hides the heavens and the heavens will never show.

So I imagine it with the goodness of my mind. I suppose I must have a goodness filled mind because the heavens are never bad. So they say and I am sure that they are never wrong.

What is goodness to them, is like vegetable to me. For me, potatoes are good to eat specially when they are fried. Heaven must be a plate full of fried potatoes. I wish I could eat the heaven. So I chew them. Hot. They watch me chew and laugh at me. This is because they are not chewing any potato.

I stop chewing and look up at the heaven again. The clouds stay.

2

The Rainbow

Today Anna will not come. So I need not turn my eyes towards the gate; although I feel good to wait for her everyday. Time is too long to get expended when I have nothing else to do for the rest of the day.

Anna has been coming here since my mother was taken ill and was trying to make some arrangement for me. I could hear their hearts speaking out to each other. The concerned heart of my mother and the understanding heart of Anna.

The feeble and sick heart of mother with the stronger heart of Anna. The bluish heart of mother talking to the reddened heart of Anna, forming a rainbow of words about me. I could also see those rainbows of words colour my heart with their magic paint. The hearts colouring my heart. I began to love the coloured heart of mine.

"Hello!" said the red coloured heart.

"Hello!" replied the rainbow colours in my heart.

"I shall be your friend from today", said the red heart.

"I shall be your friend from today", echoed the rainbow of my heart.

"He echoes the words that are addressed to him", sighed the blue heart in an apologetic way, which was so heavy, that the rainbow in my heart began to melt out as if they would leave me and evaporate.

To check it, I sighed out too. They started to go away through my nose. I breathed them again and pulled them back. I breathed out and threw them away. It became an organized game and I laughed out aloud.

Mother sighed again. This time even louder.

3

Dreams of Day and Night

The ghost. It visited me last evening just when I had given up. It is usually never late. I suppose, it has no other place to visit. It has been visiting me since I had lost my dream.

I had a special dream, which I could bring back to me anytime and anywhere. I would dream of a talking starfish which would swim in the air around me whenever I felt lonely. I could change its colours whenever I got bored.

If I wished it to be blue, it turned blue. If I thought it to have the colour of the sun, it became a luminous gold starfish. It even made a shadow around me while it moved. I played with that shadow for a while till I got tired of it and wished it to go.

The ghost never changes its position. It never comes by day, but when night comes around the house with the spread of black, I look at the dark ceiling of my room. When the whole room becomes a great big shadow I see the ghost. It just stays there, till Anna switches on the light.

I get angry with Anna and make a noise. But she does not understand. She gives me a book to colour and sits by my side. I colour the page black.

"What have you done!" she giggles.

"What have you done!" I repeat. I do not giggle. I try to stare at the black page but do not see the ghost.

I shall lock the door tomorrow so that Anna cannot come. I could see the ghost then for a longer while.

4

Jaundice Yellow

> "When he was a small boy,
> He fell down in a pan.
> Since the pan was hot on fire,
> He made a jump and ran.
> He ran fast and fast until,

THE MIND TREE

On a stone he fell,
So he lost his very mind
And is never well."

The words came to me from a tree which had lost its leaves. I tried to find its face and could not see where it was. I needed to find one as without a face, how could it talk?

So I took the two black marks on its trunk as the eyes. One mark was bigger than the other and gave it a winking look. For the mouth, I found a longitudinal mark, a little below its left eye. The smile looked very crooked. But it would do well with the words which it was saying.

Men too have crooked smiles, specially when they see someone in a soup. My Aunt Bulbul had such a smile. When my mother was trying to teach me some lesson, from a children's text, when I was still a boy, when I could not learn, when mother had lost some of her patience, when the room had turned yellow as the jaundice I had two months back, Aunt Bulbul had the crooked smile which I could see, before she turned yellow. Jaundice yellow. The yellow was all around the room. I could also taste the yellow. That is how I learnt that yellow tasted sour.

I remember the yellow with such intensity, that my mouth starts to feel sour thinking of it. I spit the yellow out as I stare at the smiling tree.

'Smiling tree, when you tease,
Do not forget, you lost your leaves.'

The moment I think of these words, the yellow colour goes. I get back my taste.

5

Merry Gold and Shoe Flowers

Cows are never in any hurry.

When the gate was kept open by the gardener by mistake, one such cow pushed her way inside and began to lunch with the bright orange merry gold. I suppose she wanted to taste the red shoe flowers also. So she left the merry gold half way. I watched her with my great wonder. I wondered which tasted better, the merry gold or the shoe flower.

I walked near the merry gold and plucked one. I ate it with the motive of experimenting. The cow was not at all bothered even though I was so near to her. I next tasted the shoe flower. "Not bad," I concluded.

The cow gave a loud call, perhaps to thank me for joining her. I imitated her, not that perfectly as she did. But I hoped to do some practice to get the sound. The cow never laughed as men do. She was not much bothered about my imperfection. May be because there is only one sound in the cow's voice. Wish men too had one universal word in their speech.

Our "moos" brought Anna running out. She hushed the cow from the shoe flowers. The cow was not at all in a hurry to leave. She walked next to the other side, where the rows of zinnia were planted.

While Anna chased and ran, while the cow dodged her around, I had two more merry gold.

Merry gold tasted better than shoe flowers!

6

Black, Purple, and Yellow

I think the ghost is sick since its colour has changed from black to purple. But it is easier for me to spot it, as I do not have to strain my eyes to see it.

It cannot talk, but it communicates in a strange way, which is very different from what Anna says or my mother says. It assures me with a strange hope. I begin to hope that one day I will be ready to understand it completely.

Silence of the ghost makes me imagine every possible word coming out from it. Those words are not as specific as Anna's or the postman's or my mother's. They can be anything like the mooing of the cow, with whom I had feasted on the shoe flower and the merry gold. They can be the continuous hiss like that coming out from a pressure cooker, or the sound of complete silence.

Silence has a definite sound. You hear your mind talking to you. You can recall all those sounds which you either liked or you hated to hear. You can hear the black and purple getting mixed up. You can hear the crooked smile of Aunt Bulbul and you can see the yellow colour burying you, till you see only yellow. Jaundice yellow around you. The black and purple are no more seen.

The ghost is also surrounded by yellow. I do not see it anymore.

I get the taste of sourness in my mind.

7

Reflection

The clock which had been on the wall of the sitting room, ever since I had known of the world, never works. I do not know when it had last worked. But I have grown very fond of it as it is so similar to me.

It never expects anything from anyone. Neither do I. I think that no one expects anything from it or from me. We are just a part of the whole scene.

I have begun to stare at the clock. I found a great story revealed when I saw the reflection of the window grills on it. The clock has become a storyteller since then. No human being has been a storyteller to me thinking that I would not understand. I do not expect it either from any body.

But when I stare at the reflection on the glass of the clock, I can see a story. Of course, no one knows anything about it.

Only today for instance, the clock told me how reflections are born.

"When long ago, the waters never reflected the sky and the sun, when no one knew how he looked like, when the sky wondered whether it was black or blue, and the sun did not know whether to send golden rays or white rays to the earth, there was total confusion around. If you cannot see yourself, how will you be your best? So the waters and oceans of all the world, decided to give up their own colours and show the sun and the sky how they looked.

Hence, after a long day, when the sun got bored of being yellow, it turned orange and then to red. The sky too got tired of being blue and turned black."

I have told the story to no one as yet, because the clock may understand me, the tree may understand me, but not man.

Thus stories and secrets are reflected and counter reflected be
tween me and the glass of the clock.

8

If Fishes Flew

What would happen if fishes flew?

David had a book which had the picture of a fish standing up and talking to a frog. I did not read, as I was not expected to read. The words that they said formed a kind of
pattern in my mind.

For instance, when David was reading about the fish who
greeted its friend frog, I saw a patch of purple forming slowly
in front of my mind. Grape purple. I could smell the grapes too.

To make myself sure of the fact that when fishes greeted
frogs, it became grapes, I took the book from David and
sniffed. David cried out in alarm. I think, that he thought I
would harm his book. So he took it from me and ran back
home. He never brought back any book to our house.

Of course, David is a big man now. But I still ponder
over the thought of the smell of grapes when fishes greeted
frogs. I can never be sure of it.

Once I had drawn a fish to check it. I could not find out. So I drew another fish and then another. For a few days I just drew fishes. To encourage me in my new skill, my mother gave me more pages. I drew more fishes till I got frustrated with my drawings. But whenever I had the pencil in my hand, I drew a fish although I wanted to draw a star. And then I had the wonderful dream of the starfish. The dream came back to me over and over again, whether I slept or awoke. It changed colours at my will.

That is how I came to know that starfishes can fly if I wished. And what would happen if fishes flew? Nothing would.

9

Invisible Porcupine

There must be a great porcupine on the roof. Invisible porcupine. Otherwise why should I hear it? The bristles made such a sound, that I did not sleep at all. Of course, it was not intending to do any harm. It was just being a little noisy, that's all. I think, it wanted to play with me. Sometimes animals just do not understand the relativeness of time!

I tried to tell it that mother has the keys of the door and

she keeps the door locked at night after that day, when I had found the moon in the garden.

I had opened the latch of the door to bring the moon inside. If mother had not woken up, I could have the moon for myself. Of course, I would not have been selfish and kept it for me. I would definitely have let it out at the evenings for the world to share. But I would have let it out by tying a long string to it so that, I could bring it back during the day before anyone got up.

The porcupine was too big to keep inside the house. I was sure that mother would not like it. How about giving it a trim in the bristles? But the animal was an invisible one and so I had to think of some other way to befriend it.

The moon was shining with a curved look in the sky. Did it see the porcupine on the roof? It never told me any thing!

Perhaps it was too obvious to tell.

I wondered how I did not know anything about it until last night.

10

Worry

Long long ago, when nothing was there, and God got bored with Himself, He made everything. Then He got bored of everything that was perfect and planned to make some distortions. So He made some like me who as they say have lost their minds.

Of course there was nothing to worry for it, because as they say we cannot worry and fret. They are not wrong because they have not lost their minds. So I do not worry, although I tried to worry and feel for myself what worrying could be like.

At first I had looked at the sun and tried to worry. It hurt my eyes and so I shifted my eyes to the tree. The tree which had the crooked smile. It hurt me with the colour yellow. Jaundice yellow. Next I saw myself looking at the sky. The blue of the sky was smiling at me. I was sure that it was not worrying me any bit.

Then I could feel an uncertain fear when I stared at my reflection into the mirror. I could feel my image getting molten till the mirror became one whole opaque wall and I began to doubt my vision. At that moment I knew how to get worried.

When you saw your reflection melt and when the whole mirror turns opaque, when you doubt your vision, you can be sure to get worried. Of course, worrying is never transparent. The sky is transparent and the heaven is in the sky. So the heaven is never worried. Hence, God is not worried.

I am not worried too, although I know how to look at the mirror and get worried.

11

A Moo of Pain

The cow with whom I had the feast of merry gold and shoe flowers had peeped in the morning to check whether the gate was open or not. I could have opened it for her, but I was afraid that Anna would chase her out again. How would you like your guest to be treated?

I had a picture book when I was a boy. It had the picture of a cow. I have lost it long back. No one buys picture books for me any more. I think men do not get picture books. But surely I would love to have one.

The cow had waited for me to open the gate for a while and then left. I had mooed out aloud as cows have only one word in their vocabulary. When they are hungry, they moo. When they greet each other, they moo. They moo in pain and in happiness.

I had felt bad when I did not open the gate for her. When you lose your mind, you have to follow some rules which those who have not lost their minds set for you. For instance, I am not supposed to touch the cassette player, I am not supposed to come out into the drawing room when guests are around, I am not supposed to call any cow inside the house however gentle the cow may be, I am not supposed to eat shoe flowers.

There are many more things people of my age like David do, which I am not supposed to do.

I felt helpless inside me somewhere near the eyes. Tears ran down because I had lost a friend.

I mooed in pain.

12

Transparency

Suddenly things have become all transparent. A transparent room, then a transparent ceiling, a transparent house, a transparent shape of Anna walking in and out of the room, a transparent sun through which I could see a red heart of the sun throbbing and a transparent reflection of myself showing only the rainbow colours of my heart. That is how I came to know that all things can be transparent, but not the heart.

Mother's heart was purple today but when she held her chest and coughed, the heart turned yellow. Cough yellow. I could not find any heart when I stared at the transparency of the tree which had the crooked smile.

One thing was for sure that when I tried to find the reason why I saw transparent things, I noticed that the day was a very special one. The earth was celebrating its birthday. I marked the date on a transparent calendar, with a transparent pen, which had transparent ink.

It was not until evening that I realized how difficult it was to live in the transparent world because I kept faltering my steps when I tried to climb. I hurt my toes twice and then decided not to go upstairs.

Nobody expected me to go up either. It made no difference whether I stayed downstairs or went upstairs. It did make me wonder about the transparent world which I could probably see better if I went up.

Anna found me crawling up the stairs. She helped me climb up. I saw her red heart throb faster.

13

This or That

Many things can happen in a minute. This or that; some of this and some of that; all of this and none of that; or all of that and none of this. It depends on which you consider important, this or that.

It was just last night, when I was having my dinner, and watching the television, wondering, when the world would sleep and the porcupine would settle down on the roof, so that I could guess it move, I had noticed a wall lizard chasing a flying insect.

When things are stationary around you, your eyes are bound to get attracted by any movement. And what a movement it was!

The movement of hunger behind the food, the movement of death chasing life, the movement which would result either to this or to that. I did not interfere. When movements of that kind takes place, you should not interfere. The lizard had power but the insect had wings. "Fair enough", I reasoned. Of course, my reasoning have no value to them, for I have lost my mind as they say. That may be "Fair enough", too. I am no judge.

So I concentrated on the movement which was taking place. Death finally overtook life. The room was the same, the walls were the same. Why, I was still having my food and the food tasted the same. Yet the death had taken place and it made no difference to any one.

I wondered about life, all through the night. The porcupine on the roof was also silent.

May be it too thought.

14

When Street Dogs Bark

I had scratched my ears long back when I was a boy. I had heard a street dog bark at that moment. So I had realized that when your ears scratched, street dogs barked.

From that day onwards, I made it a point to scratch my ears whenever I heard street dogs barking. But I certainly got doubtful if I saw people around me not paying any attention to street dogs' barks.

Once or twice, I took somebody's hands to his ears to remind him about it. But nobody could understand me.

Somebody had even thought that I wanted to play with him. So he held his ears and tried to pretend being a cat and chased me around the table. It had made me all the more upset.

Of course, it happened long back when the house was filled with people and noise. Yet, the barking dogs are always there and they remind me that it is time for me to scratch my ears.

The other day, when I was holding a cup full of tea, there was a little mishap. I had heard a dog bark somewhere and immediately took my hands to my ears. I did not realize that the cup will fall and break. Anna was upset. Very upset.

I was more upset. It was the cup which I had loved the most. The blue pieces on the spilled tea looked dead on the tea coloured blood. That is how I learnt that when you break and die, your blood becomes tea coloured.

The dog had stopped barking. Anna was picking up the blue pieces. Cling-clong. The cup was dead.

15

Yes and No

"Yes, I am sure he has touched my bag. Ask him."
Anu was furious as her purse was missing. "Did I do it?" I had asked myself.

'No', said my mind.

"Yes", said my mouth when she looked at me fiercely and asked.

I did not mean to say "yes" or "no". But I was so used to saying "yes", that I said it to avoid any other dialogue. Her eyes hurt me even though she had worn her glasses and her face was turning into that of a frog's face. The frog which was being greeted by a fish. But since the fish was not there, grape purple could not form.

The room had a black mattress on which there was a print of a shoe which was definitely not mine. Yet she would confirm. So mother asked me to remove my shoes and measured it. I was lucky. The mark on the mattress was bigger than the size of my shoe.

I was feeling the sour taste return to my mouth with humiliation. But then I remembered that boys like me have no right to be humiliated. It made no difference whether I was glorified or whether I was humiliated.

I was standing there watching the room turn yellow. Jaundice yellow, which was covering away every thing till I could only see the shoe imprint challenging my eyes.

I turned away my face from the yellow scene.

"Why did you tell 'yes', when you meant to say 'no'?" Mother had asked me.

"Yes", I replied, as the world was gaining back the colours.

16

The Image of the Ghost

The ghost looked bluish this evening and I was able to see its eyes too, although I had to strain my eyes a bit. When it was black, I could only guess its face.

There is an advantage in guessing. You have a great deal of possibilities to choose from. You can be more creative and also you can change your thoughts according to the mould of your different moods. Otherwise, things can be too obvious and get boring.

For instance my own face. It has the same colour and the same shape which I see every day except those days, when it gets transparent. Of course, it has changed to a great extent from what it was when I was a boy. The change was too slow for me to get interested.

Did the ghost realize that its colour was changing? I think that ultimately it will take the colour white as all ghosts are expected to be white.

I wanted to show it its reflection, since I could see its eyes. So I brought down the great mirror from the wall along with the cobwebs, along with a lizard which was resting behind it, and along with it, a ton of dust. I carefully placed it on the floor, so that the ghost could see how it looked. But the mirror either did not show the reflection, to the ghost, or the ghost could not identify its shadow. It just stared at me as if I was more interesting rather than its image.

Anna as usual came in to switch on the light and spoil the evening. She scolded me for bringing down the mirror from the wall.

While she was putting it back, I realized that the mirror was turning opaque.

17

Mango Face

If mangoes had eyes, nose and mouth, they would look like him.

He came and asked for my mother. He asked me as I was sitting outside waiting. Of course, I was not sure for whom I was waiting. It could be any body, the cow, the postman or the gardener or even those sun coloured butterflies which had visited me last morning. So I was not sure.

But when the mango faced man came in and asked for my mother I just sat and watched him. He obviously thought that I did not understand or hear him. So he asked me again if I could call my mother.

I did not move and kept staring at the gate. How can a person who had lost his mind call? I began to wonder about different ways of calling. But how does a butterfly call? No, I did not know the answer.

I needed to find out, and so decided to ask the story telling clock. I got up and walked in. Mango face thought that I got up to call my mother and stood at the door. I do not know what happened to him after that or for how long he had been waiting.

I was in for a greater quest to find out how butterflies called. Lest I forget, I decided to fly inside to the clock.

So I flapped my hands to go inside. But I was not flying like butterflies. So I hopped my way along. It was clumsy, but I knew now what I was waiting for.

Mango face waited too.

18

When Butterflies Sang

"Many days ago, when the sun was bigger than what it is now, when the sky was coloured in the rainbow hue, butterflies were born. They were born from the rainbow of the sky.

"Red butterflies, from the red of the rainbow, blue butter-flies, from the blue of the rainbow, and yellow ones, from the yellow colour of the rainbow." The clock paused for a while.

I wanted to ask the clock about how the spotted butter-flies were born, but thought it wise not to disturb it.

"When they were born, each butterfly could sing as sweetly as a cuckoo." The clock showed me the reflection of the rainbow sky and the millions of fluttering butterflies com-ing out from there.

"One day there was a great competition. Competitions are bound to take place when there are too many talents around and when you feel the urge to prove your worth. You need to feel a winner so that your ego is satisfied."

But the clock told me not to worry, as those who have lost their minds need not have egos. I was relieved.

I saw in the glass of the clock, butterflies performing. The whole earth under the rainbow sky resonating with the tune. Even the sun had mellowed down by the children of the rainbow sky.

"Birds came down from all their nests and trees to find out what was happening. Nobody likes to have better and more talented people around. So, the birds out of petty jeal-ousy, attacked the butterflies. Many insects were eaten up by the birds that day. Since that day butterflies never use their voices even to call out.

"Displaying can welcome trouble." The clock finished.

19

Black and Blue

When you are trying to think blue but end up thinking of black, you can be sure to get frustrated. Time and again, it happens to me and I am sure that I get quite helpless. Otherwise, why should I get up and spin myself?

Spinning my body brings some sort of harmony to my thoughts so that I can centrifuge away all the black thoughts. I have realized that faster I spin, faster it gets to drive away the black.

After spinning for a while, when I become sure that even the last speck of black has gone away from me, then I spin back in the opposite direction and pull the blue thoughts into myself. It depends on me how much of blue I want.

If I want more blue, I have to spin faster. Otherwise not so fast.

That is exactly what I was doing when my mother came into the scene. She sighed her usual heavy breath, pumping out all the volume of air out of her.

When I was a boy, she used to stop me whenever I spun out a thought. Now she does not any more. I saw the heaviness of her breath coming out as a smoke of sick blue. So I had to stop spinning myself because there were chances that I would pull in the sick blue.

There was no other way to think blue. The silent blue which I wanted to think about could not be pulled within.

I remained with my colourless thoughts.

20

Picture of My Father

The picture on the entrance of our house, which is hung at an angle to face the main door, is that of my father's.

It reflects the main door and anyone who enters through it, gets reflected. I have seen the boy who delivers milk, comb his hair, seeing his reflection in it.

Mother never looks at it. I often wonder why.

But the clock has told me one day that when men become pictures, they hurt. So I tried to stare at the unblinking eyes of my father's picture, and tried to get hurt. Nothing happened. Perhaps I could not remember anything of him, when his eyes used to blink.

But I definitely wonder what it would have been like, if he

was to be around. Of course, he would have been an old man now and would have sighed perhaps like my mother does. What could have been the colour of his sighs? Would it have the sick blue colour like that of my mother's or something more bright?

But I could not come to any solution by merely seeing the picture, as it never breathes or sighs.

What was he like?

Was he like Aunt Bulbul's husband, who just sits in the drawing room and reads? Or was he like next door David's father, who spends his time with the big white dog?

Questions and more questions leads to guessing and further guessing leading the thoughts to nowhere.

It is that "Nowhere" which gives birth to dreams and desires.

It is that "Nowhere" where all dreams and desires fall back!

21

Black Thoughts

Anu was walking slowly to her room in the special school, which I attended when I was a boy. It was the day after when she had accused me of entering her room and stealing money from her cupboard.

The day was a gray coloured one because the sun had not been out from behind the smoke like clouds, which had the whole width of the sky to themselves.

Anu had passed by. And she had spread the jaundice yellow all over the place as she passed by. The grass became jaundice yellow, the air became jaundice yellow and the stones around became infected by the jaundice yellow too.

Soon I could see nothing else but the shoes which she had asked me to remove so that she could measure it with the marks on the black mattress of her therapy room. My brown shoes hanging on the jaundice yellow. A sea of jaundice yellow. With it, came a flood of sour saliva in my mouth. I spitted it out and all the black thoughts came to my mind.

I sat on the swing of the school's playground to push away the black thoughts and jerked my body with the forward and backward motion of the swing.

The problem with the black thoughts is that, they refuse to go easily. The spots of black remain, even though you try to jerk them away. They will remain distinct and also may threaten to engulf the other thoughts with their limitless darkness.

The gray clouds of the sky touched those black thoughts, while jaundice yellow spilled around in bounty.

22

Happiness and Sorrow

"In a dark place called Somewhere, there lived happiness. Happiness was too contented with itself to spread out, and so it remained in that place called 'Somewhere'. Somewhere, was a place of paradise of happiness.

"One day from 'Nowhere' came Sorrow to the place called Somewhere. But as there was Happiness around, Sorrow could not find home. So it was asked to leave the place called Somewhere.

"Sorrow went back to Nowhere from where it had come from. But who would now keep Sorrow back? So Sorrow occupied the hearts of people who were kind and compassionate as they never refused to give it place to stay.

"If your heart aches when you see a tear in someone's eyes, if your eyes burn when someone is wrongly accused, if you feel the pain, which a person who has lost his mind bears, if you are ready to accept such a person and help him, you can be sure that you have sheltered sorrow in your heart. So you feel it and understand it.

"Happiness from the place called Somewhere has to be bought as it is expensive. Sorrow comes free of cost. That is why the poor cannot afford Happiness as easily as Sorrow.

Sorrow can be found anywhere other than Somewhere and Nowhere.

> "A heart full of laughter
> Is often costlier.
> So I kept a tear
> For ever and forever."

The clock thus told me the secret of Happiness and Sorrow.

23

Waiting

The lizard has many homes. It lives behind the big mirror which I had brought down to show the ghost what it looked like when it was blue; it also lives behind the Story telling clock; I have also seen it peeping from behind the picture of my father. So it never gets bored.

I stay in the same house and try to feel the same independence as it feels. Yet I cannot feel it. I suppose, when you lose your mind, you cannot accept the same sort of independence which others around you, who have not lost their minds, can accept.

I concentrated on the movement of the lizard. There was no insect around for it to chase at that moment. It just lay flat on the wall with its stomach touching the surface. Yet it was waiting. I know that it was waiting.

I was waiting too, yet as usual, not sure what I waited for. Perhaps I was waiting for the lizard to move, perhaps I waited for the clouds to move, or perhaps for Anna to come and sit by me with her stitching. Maybe I was waiting for some black thought filled with jaundice yellow or a blue colour sigh of my mother.

The lizard was looking at some remote corner as it waited. I was looking at the lizard as I waited. The walls of the room were still around me and I was quite sure, that they too waited. Perhaps they like me, did not know what they waited for.

Outside the room, the sun waited to see the earth and the clouds waited for the air to push them away. The earth must be waiting too to find a reason as to why it had to move; while life on the earth waited for the certainty of death.

The lizard lay still. Flat on its stomach.

24

Grayish Loneliness

The colour of loneliness is gray.

When I was sitting and waiting for the cow to come and moo at the gate, as it sometimes does, I realized that, I felt lonely.

The moment I realized it, things started to change their colours. Not that they did not retain their actual colours, but they became grayish.

For instance, the sun was golden but grayish. The sky was blue, but grayish. My shirt was yellow, but grayish. The tree which has the crooked smile and without any leaves, was brown, but grayish.

Anna who was talking to the postman, had some grayish coloured words for me to breathe in. When I breathed them I could feel those grayish words, flow along with my blood all over my body. I knew that my blood was red, but a little grayish.

I was in fact enjoying this grayish loneliness because gray was a soft colour. It never covered up the other colours like the devouring jaundice yellow.

It was at that moment that I had realized, that gray tasted sweet. I opened my mouth to taste the sweet gray and fill myself with its sweetness.

The cow never turned up that day although I had mooed twice. But when I mooed, I found all those words which Anna spoke, which I had pulled in, start coming out with the grayish moos.

I stopped mooing, lest I lose the filling gray from myself.

25

Bubbled Words

"I do not think that he is benefitting from this school." The teacher had told mother.

'Here we go again.' I told myself and pushed aside the words by wiping the air.

That was long back, when I was a boy and when mother did not send out the sick blue sighs.

That was, I think my last school.

"Why should boys like me need schools? After all how can we be taught, since we had lost our minds?"

Mother had requested. What else could she do?

"Won't you reconsider?" She had asked.

"Sorry", came the reply.

I waved all the words which they said, and watched the

words toss in the air like bubbles of soap all around me. They arranged and rearranged themselves all around and I laughed aloud.

"See, why I told you," the teacher told my mother pointing towards me. I played all along with those words, as their numbers increased while they spoke.

It was later that I had found out that words had colours and how those colours can diffuse through each other and cover you up.

Now I do not laugh when words fly like soap bubbles except when they form a rainbow cover in my heart. I do not play with them by waving them away but try to feel them by breathing them in and out.

I had walked out of the school, with a tail of words following me.

Words made of letters, crawling like ants, in a disciplined row.

26

Pink Smile

I have a new set of crayons to colour today. Whenever Unkle Ahmed visits us, he brings a set of colours for me. I have a collection of colours, since I have been getting them from my boyhood times.

Sometimes, when I am breathing in the lonely gray, and when everything turns grayish, I sit with my crayons and pages to colour them. So I colour a tree green, but grayish. I colour the sun yellow, but grayish.

"Why are you spoiling the beautiful sun with that gray?" Anna asks me.

"Why are you spoiling the beautiful sun with that gray." I reply.

Next time Anna is more careful. She hides the gray colours from all the sets.

The lonely gray is made lonely by Anna.

> In some distant far away,
> Lonely gray goes astray.

The colours were given to me by Unkle Ahmed. He was my father's friend. He has been visiting us since my father's death. When he is at home, mother smiles so much. She forgets even to sigh. The sick blue sighs.

Unkle Ahmed had once asked me to draw something for him. I had drawn a pink page with a pink sun and a pink star although I knew very well that sun and stars do not come out at the same time.

My mother has a pink smile whenever Unkle Ahmed

visits us. So I look forward to his visits. When mother smiles pink, she looks so pretty. My pink coloured page cannot get the exact pinkness which I want to show. So I try another page and then another and again another till I find the pink crayon missing.

Anna has done it again.

27

Colours Didn't Matter Anymore

The ghost has not changed its colour since a long time now. It is fixed with blue. I had once wished it to be a "balloon blue" colour, but it did not matter any more.

The starfish was different. It understood all my wishes and did them. But everything should be different. So I can just wish of a balloon blue ghost and not expect anything from it. It never expects anything from me either. It has never asked me to look at it and wait for it when the room turns to a big shadow and the evening turns black.

For a few days, I did not look up purposely expecting it to call me or make some indication to draw my attention. It did nothing, although I knew that it was very much there.

Finally I had given up, and looked up at it. It was neither happy nor sad. It neither smiled nor blinked. Yet it made me feel relieved by its presence. There was no word from it. Yet it assured me that it will be there, if I looked up for it.

So, when the sun goes down and the great black shadow spreads in the room and beyond it, when the smile of the smiling tree cannot be seen any more, when the sick blue sigh of my mother is covered with black, I can find the ghost if and only if I wanted to.

It had made itself clear through its silent stare, it was all up to me. Whether I wanted to see it or not as it was.

I had accepted it finally for what it was whether it was blue, whether it was black or, whether it was purple.

28

Realization

> 'When he started growing up
> Something sure he missed,
> So he spends time with lonely gray,
> And is a misfit!'

When these straight forward words came from the tree with a crooked smile, I was strangely not upset any more.

The jaundice yellow did not cover my eyes to shade away the truth.

I realized something sure was wrong with me. Otherwise, why should I miss out on the many things which people of my age did? Why should mother sigh the sick blue breath when she saw me? Why should I get removed from one school, and then another, and then another?

Yet I never would be able to understand the exact reason for my difference.

When you have to do the guessing on yourself and about yourself, you become worried. You can see yourself melting when you stand in front of the mirror.

Even though, I realize that I am not expected to be worried, yet I just cannot help.

The tree with the crooked smile, does not look as crooked as before. I touch it with tenderness, and wish to spend my gray times with it. I spread my hands up like its two branches spreading my fingers, as much as their flexibility would permit me. I stood there for a long while.

I had never before felt so peaceful. The colour of peace, I realized was orange brown as I saw the orange brown setting sun's rays light the topmost branches of the tree. The tree with a crooked smile and straight words.

Jaundice yellow had gone forever, never to haunt me again.

29

To the Greenish Hope

"Can nothing be changed with me?" I ask the clock which tells me stories.

"Yes, things can be changed," tells the clock.

But I understand that somethings need waiting. I get ready to wait for the green colour of hope which would cover me all through. There may be different colours around me, but the clock told me that everything will be greenish. The transparent earth will be greenish, the transparent sun will show a greenish transparency, the blue heart of my mother will be blue but be greenish, loneliness will be gray and yet be greenish, my heart too when Anna or mother spoke, would have the rainbow colours and yet be greenish.

The clock showed me the reflection of that "would be greenish" world, which was so fulfilling, that I wished I could be on the other side of its glass. The whole morning, I wondered how that greenish world would be like. It would make me feel better in a greenish way.

During the afternoon I had thought so much about green hope, that I coloured a few pages green. I had locked the door, so that Anna could not enter and hide the green crayons from my set.

Both Anna and mother were upset and worried about me. They pleaded and knocked the door hard and then harder. I was not going to open the door again and let the greenish hope leave me. I saw the greenish red drops of blood gushing out of my wrist. Yes, it pained. But since it was a green pain, I did not mind much. The blue heart of my mother echoed in my fading rainbow greenish heart before my eyes closed to a transparent greenish world.

And I could go across to the other side of the glass in the clock.

The Mind Tree

one

Mind Tree

It is very dark around. May be it is night, or may be it is day. I cannot be sure because I am not yet feeling the heat of the sun. Only when the sun throws heat, I get to know that it is day. So I make myself prepared for the moment when someone will come.

Moments come and go. But they make you wait long. And when the expected moment comes you are so overwhelmed by the presence of it that you forget to react the way you had planned to do. So you let the moment go like all the other moments which have gone past you. Where did they go after all? In some nowhere which is invisible to all those who are being in the moment of present.

Yet I know that 'Nowhere' exists within my own mind which keeps coming to me whenever I try to search the mind of mine. For instance, when I had been gifted this mind of mine, I recall 'his' voice very clearly.

To you I have given this mind,
And you shall be the only kind,
For no one ever will like you be,
And I name you the Mind Tree.

I know my name since that moment. Who he was I do not know, as he had gifted me just this mind. I cannot see or talk. So I could never ask anybody who he was.

Yet I can imagine. I can hope and I can expect. I am able to feel the pains but I cannot cry. So I just be and wait for the pain to subside. I can do nothing else but wait.

The silence around tells me that it is night. I wait for the day.

two

The Crow Feeder

I wish I knew how I looked like. The more I wonder the more I get my mind exhausted with the never-ending guesses of mine. It is true that my branches spread far from my main trunk and my leaves are broad. It is also true that I give shade to people. So the hot afternoons of my life are never lonely.

When the sun throws all its heat on the earth, when the earth around begins to crack, when the life on earth breathes hot air, when the dust blows with the wind and when the crows settle down on my branches, I can make out that it is midday.

I know that it is the time when the crow feeder will come. He comes and sits under my shade. I can hear him humming a tune. He hums louder when he is happy. Yesterday his hum was soft. I could sense that he was sad. I was sad too. I wanted to ask him why he sang so softly. But I am just a Mind Tree. I have been gifted this mind. I can hope, I can imagine, I can love but I cannot ask. My concerns and worries are trapped within me somewhere in my depths, may be in my roots, may be in my bark or may be all around my radius. I just wonder.

I know him and yet so much of him is unknown. So I can only shape him with my imagination. As he feeds the crows, as he calls them fondly, as the crows quarrel for a last bit and make the afternoon the most cawing filled afternoon, I wonder and wonder. I wonder how his amused face would look like, I wonder whether he has eaten any thing or has fed everything to the cawing birds.

Who he is does not matter any more as I try to fan him with my broad leaves of my lowest branch. I sense him lying under me as his breaths get heavier.

He sleeps.

three

And Night Around

The stars of night,
With trembling light,
In the distant far,
Wish I had sight,
To see their light
And talk to those twinkling stars!

When the sun goes down and the earth grows quiet in a deep penance, when the life around breathes the cool west wind, when the leaves of my branches whisper with each other with a shushing hiss, when the birds return to sleep for the night in their nests and when some distant night bird hoots, I can sense the starlight on me piercing even through my thick bark.

I never sleep as I am never tired. My mind works in the stillness of the night as each leaf of mine breathes in the dark night air.

A reptile crosses my roots with idle ripples of a chill body while I feel its cold length crossing my anchoring roots. I feel its movements with envy. Any movement makes me envious. I wonder where it could go.

Its idle movement tells that it is not going after any prey. It is perhaps out because of its nocturnal habit of taking a stroll in the darkness. I begin to follow it mentally.

Did it cross the abandoned house to my right side across which lies the stretch of uncultivated land which echoes the bleats of the goats during the day? Did it go beyond the field towards the east where a little village lies, or did it take the way towards the railway track through which the trains pass trembling the very earth with resonance?

I wonder and wonder while the night around lies with usualness. Stars around the sky drop their light to touch my heart which is as unobjective as my mind. My heart then collects all that light and spreads it all along my body into the depth of my roots.

The earth sucks all of it from my roots and feels the blessings of the stars.

four

Happy Men

> Happiness of men does spread
> All around the path they tread.

A group of men sometimes sit under my shade when the sun shows the late afternoon hour. They are five in number. Sometimes one or two more join them.

I can tell that they are coming, from their happy laughter which come as a cheerful wave from a distance. When they come, I try to get myself prepared to welcome them. They fill the stillness of the surroundings with such happiness that even the world seems to be a round ball of laughter.

I try to wave my branches and leaves with vigour even though there is no wind helping me. Of course, I have to make an extra effort to move my branches without any help from the wind. Yet I think that my welcome gets unnoticed as the happy men sit under my shadow and talk.

They bring wine with them and slowly get themselves drunk. I listen to them with amusement. It is not a very polished kind of entertainment, I must admit. Yet when their speech gets slurred, when their words come out with louder blows, when jokes turn to abuses, when abuses turn to swears and when swears lead to quarrels, I know that it is because of that magic liquid which they have been drinking.

One of them try to sing. Another one encourages him by clapping his hands. The third one tries to stagger around my thick trunk and dance. While the next one just gets bored and falls asleep. The fifth one watches them. The empty bottle rolls around and gets kicked by a pair of dancing feet.

My leaves always cheer the happy men by clapping each other loudly.

The sun slowly cools down to remind the happy men that the earth needs rest. They stagger their steps slowly leaving the empty bottle rolling around. The air smells of their sweat and wine. The earth turns quiet once more as the sound of their feet becomes fainter and fainter to merge with the other sounds.

My mind follows them.

five

Living World

> The world as a whole, is a living self
> And breeds all the life I can tell.

The world is a breathing life form in itself. Does it have a mind like I have? In that case, where does it keep its mind?

Sometimes I feel certain that the world does have a mind of its own. It can understand much more than what it shows. You need not show off your understanding when you do not want to be disturbed, and when you are satisfied with your state.

When you are satisfied with yourself, only then you can be as peaceful as that field which lies on the other side, where the goat-herds come from the sleepy village to graze their goats. The bleats of the animals make a gentle wave in the wind while I try to take in that sound with my leaves which vibrate with each bleat.

The earth listens too. I am certain of it. It listens with a great satisfaction as I can feel it under my deep roots. But it never shows any of it to anybody. Why should it? When it is all around us, we take it for granted. We do all our deeds good and bad on its heart. It accepts the good and it accepts the bad without any judgement. It never shows that it is hurt. Isn't it enough to prove that it is enjoying a deep satisfaction somewhere deep within?

Yet I have sensed it getting hurt. When a fire had broken one night, on that sleepy village and when the fire had spread into the houses, when a calf which was newly born could not keep pace with its running mother and got burnt before her helpless eyes, when she had called out to the calf for the last time, I had sensed the earth sigh with great pain. Otherwise, why should my leaves and branches shake when there was no wind?

I had sighed too, as I could smell the fire even from here. It was a moment I had wished that I had no mind at all. I was as helpless as the earth. A little chick in its nest somewhere on my branches woke up when I had sighed. I promised myself to be gentle next time.

The village on the heart of the earth burnt.

six

Ants

Little selves in busy way
Make the best of their day.

Ants have started making themselves busy since morning. I can feel them crawling up and down my trunk and branches heading for the ripe fruit that has cracked open to disperse the ripe seeds.

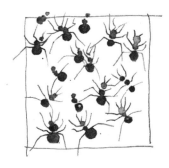

Ants had followed the scent and found the ripe fruit. I could sense their constancy of speed which was like a continuous flow of life. A long thread of life seeking the ripe fruit and a second long thread of life coming down. An organised form of life form having the same goal.

There was however a fight when a rival group of ants had come from somewhere to share the ripe fruit. The war did not last long. I could sense the attempts of pushing and crawling on each other. The movements could hardly tickle me. Yet I knew that it was an important war.

Trees like me fight too. When a creeper once, long back, tried to take its roots just below me, I had dropped some branches on it to warn it. But the creeper could not understand my warning. All plants cannot be Mind Trees. Without mind, instincts work but not judgement. The creeper however survived for a few more days until one day, one of the goats which had come underneath me consumed it.

The fruit was covered with ants. I could feel the bites. When the pain was too much for me, I shook it down. It fell down along with the ants. Slowly the ascending and descending threads of life thinned down till I could not feel them any more.

seven

Windy Day

> All the day had a wind
> And windy quite it was
> And in the wind I had watched
> A little life was lost.

Last week there was a very windy day. I felt the wind all over my body. When the wind blew and threatened to show me its power, when I was afraid of being uprooted, when the nest on my branches swayed and rocked, when the little chicks in the nest came close to each other and when my branches fought to save the nest, the world seemed to be one whole place of confusion.

There was confusion in the air as dust blew, there was confusion among the goats as they started to run, there was confusion all around the field as the goat herds chased the goats all around the field so that they stayed together, there was confusion in the sky as the clouds came from somewhere and threatened to pour, and there was confusion in the nest because the chicks tried to escape and one of them fell on the ground.

I could hear its feeble squeaks. I realised that it had broken its leg. Yet I could do nothing to help it. The wind blew all around me that day. My branches could not bear its strength any more. I had to give up in the end.

Two of my branches broke. One of them fell on the chick, and immediately it stopped its squeaks. I had dropped the branch on its head. The little life was lost under my heavy branch. My broken body hurt and yet I could not feel it, as a terrible guilt overpowered me.

I wanted to give up my mind at that moment. The wind laughed all around me and rain started to pour. It had washed away some of my tears with it. I could guess its drops on the body of the dead bird making a pool of rain water which was stained with blood around it. I could guess the water slowly regaining its colour as there remained no more blood to flow.

I stood as a survivor with a broken nest and two terrified chicks who still did not know whether or not to trust me.

eight

The Heart of the Earth

All of the earth has a heart
In some deepest core
It beats perhaps deep and far
Since the times of yore.

As I stand on the earth, with my roots clinging on to the hardness of the earth, I can sense some movements deeper down somewhere in the core of the ground. The faint ripples get detected by my roots and I become aware that the great heart of the earth is beating somewhere down there.

I wish that my roots could go down below, further and further, till they touched the great heart. Yet there are limitations, and I have my limitations too. Every beyond is within a boundary. But not my mind when it imagines. It crosses every beyonds to touch further and further beyonds faster than any limit of time. And time is limitless too, although it limits the events within its set up boundaries.

So we measure the length of events with the standard set up by the time. Hence I could tell that the great heart of the earth beats very slowly. To realise this, it took a long time. I had to wait for the vibrations in succession, keeping my roots alert even to pick up the slightest ripple.

I could guess the great heart expanding and contracting, circulating the very essence of life all over its radius, through my roots, through that stone, through the field where the goat herds bring their goats, and through the wild air above it, to carry that life breath further and further away wherever there is the essence of that life. I could imagine the great breath of life, growing and growing, to reach the skies and get spread out to reach every flying bird that can dare the floating clouds.

Within myself, where my mind is trapped, I can feel my leaves breathing that breath of life, the same breath which every living being breathed. A snail, a man and a tree.

nine

I Guess and Hope

> All the sky is spread out far
> And is full of bliss
> Yet with sightless thoughts in self
> I guess the sights I miss.

Sometimes I feel that I should have asked for the gift of sight from him who had given my mind to me. It so happened that when he was gifting me the mind, I was so overwhelmed by the moment of it, that I had in fact forgotten even to thank him. I just stood there with the awareness that I exist and I had existed. Before that moment, I had never known anything about anything or even myself.

So when I had this gift of mind, I came to know that I am a Mind Tree and I was just a tree before. Yet my past was not revealed to me although I had tried my best to find out. When mind is absent, memories do not get recorded. So I could only depend on the self learnt fact that one day I was born when someone had planted me. Or may be a seed had dropped from some beak of a bird where my roots have taken their stand. May be my leaves escaped the goats and I grew up with no knowledge about myself.

May be this and may be that. But may be it. I tell myself as I stand below a clear sky and wonder how it looks like. I can tell that the sky is clear from the amount of sun rays which I feel. I can tell that the sky is clear from the shrieks of the eagles which encircle the field, where the goat herds come with their goats. I can tell that the sky is clear from the air around. Yet I cannot tell how the clear sky looks like as I cannot even imagine how I look like. When he comes next, I shall ask him for the gift of sight.

I doubt his return and yet hope for it. May be he will. May be he will not.

ten

Footsteps

> Footsteps from far and near
> All my waking hours I hear
> Some I am sure are too clear
> Some are strange yet sound familiar.

As I stand with my mind filled with some hopes, some memories, some doubts, some speculations, and some aspirations, I can hear footsteps. Footsteps are all around. Footsteps which are present, as well as footsteps which are heard from the depth of memories. Sometimes those footsteps merge with the recently heard ones and I hear a riddling orchestra of footsteps.

Footsteps of the goats, footsteps of the goat herds, footsteps of the happy men with the dancing feet, footsteps of the horse which comes from some yonder past whose rider used to rest below me as the crow feeder does now, footsteps of the soldiers who had killed the horse rider for some reason unknown to me, and the haunting footsteps of the frightened horse which was tied and had tried hard to escape.

I was helpless too. The horse was tied to my trunk and I could not even help it to run away. The animal had neighed out aloud for help. In those yonder days goat herds never came this way. Its master would not wake up any more. It was free and yet it could not be freed from the rope which its master had tied it with when he was alive.

The horse had given up finally as it learnt that fate overpowers destiny. Its master's body was growing with stink and had brought many jackals and scavenging birds who were still hesitating to feed on the body because of it. The horse, hungry and thirsty had guarded the body for three days, charging at any advancing beast.

Finally, the hoofs became silent and footsteps of jackals and vultures came nearer and nearer.

eleven

Spring

> And from further mist of past
> Comes her voice my near
> Lost somewhere in the maze of time
> Yet my mind does hear.

She would come with her friends and hang a swing around my lowest branch. She would jump and try to pass the other end of the rope across me. She would giggle along with her friends if she could not do it for the first time. I could hear their bangles and anklets tinkle as if they giggled after her. She would try again. With every try, the sound of her bangles and anklets would ring together. She would not give up. She would try again and again till she could do it.

And she would do it finally. I knew her name, as I heard her friends calling her. But I had a special name for her. I called her Spring!

> Like the spring she had her stay
> Like the spring she cheered
> And like spring she filled the air
> With her voice so dear.

I knew that she was pretty. I knew that she could enchant anybody including the air around her, including the dust which flew with the swing, including the sky which would gather all its clouds from somewhere, right over my head and wished that it could touch her with the raindrops.

She never stayed till the rains actually dropped. She usually left the place as suddenly as she came. She would leave with the rope swing, with her friends, with her tinkling bangles, with her anklets and with all her cheerful voice.

I would blame the sky and I would blame the time. Yet I was proud that she came to me. My lowest branch was high for her, but not as high as the sky.

I waited for the blessed moment the next day. And the monsoon poured around while the earth awaited the spring.

twelve

Hollow Footsteps

Not a soul knew of him
Not a soul like him
I think sometimes he too doubts
Of his very being.

His tired footsteps told me that he had walked quite a while. Tired footsteps are dragging. They walk for the sake of walking. The tired footsteps are of two kinds. One kind are those which aim towards some place. They walk in a direction.

The other kind of tired feet just wander. These feet are filled with hollowness. This is because the mind seeks nothing. Either the mind is absorbed in some unknown thoughts, or it is filled with a total hollowness.

I sensed a total nothingness in his thoughts. Otherwise why should he walk so undecidedly? Why should his footsteps trip on a pebble so hard and yet walk as though nothing had happened? Why should some dogs follow him and bark, while he did nothing to chase them away?

He was tired, and he was coming from the side where the village was. But I could tell that he did not belong to it. He belonged to nowhere. So he could be anywhere.

His breaths sounded neither happy nor sad. Yet they had weight of some kind of hollowness in them. As he walked, I could hear his hollow breaths following him, keeping the dogs away.

He came near me, and slowly walked under me, leaving me totally surprised. He was the only person who never even noticed me!

And the air all around
Breathed his heavy breaths,
Rest of earth lay quiet of sound,
Filled with hollowness!

thirteen

Monkeys

Monkeys come from somewhere, when my flowers dry up and when my fruits begin to grow. They sit on the roof top of the abandoned house beyond which the field lies where the goats come with the goat herds. They are about nine of them. Some years, there are one or two more.

Fathers, mothers, juveniles, cousins, aunts, sisters and infants. All in the same family.

They come first to the abandoned house to give a proper inspection whether things are in place or not. They throw some bricks here and there, all around the place. Young ones copy their fathers and are fast to learn. Babies clinging to the mothers, watch with terror and respect, as their elders show their remarkable brick aiming capabilities.

I stand and hear the bricks making a thudding sound, as they fall on the ground. When the lose bricks are done with they chase each other all around the empty rooms and the half broken roof.

The roof had broken down in a summer storm about four years back. I am sure the grandfather monkey had seen it break when he was an infant clinging to his mother.

The monkeys, during that summer storm had moved over to my branches and had clung to me with fear. I could feel, even the bravest one, with drenched body, holding on to me.

And wind around
With rains abound
Blew with mighty speed,
The flowing ground,
The raining sound,
Made bravest heart defeat.

I could feel the shivering monkeys clutch my branches, their little hearts beat fast and faster still, and when the roof of the abandoned house had broken down with a bigger roar that had dared a challenge to the thunder!

The rains had stopped after an hour's spell and the sun had come out as though to say that 'Nothing wrong had happened'. My trunk was soaking with water and I could feel the monkeys slowly come down. They had walked very cautiously to the house which stood now with a broken roof.

But this happened four years back. Every year they come with some new members to live the summer months on my branches. The crow families leave me to seek some other home.

Monkeys hang and play all around my branches, scattering twigs and half eaten fruits, chattering 'monkey language', and teaching each other monkey gestures.

fourteen

Winter Night

Silence and thoughts
Of nears and forgots
In the quiet of night
A search for lost
When absorbed
Caught in self's own plight.

When the long winter night covers the stretch of the field, on which the goats come with the goat herds during the day, when the cold wind blows the sighs of the breathing earth, when a patch of mist arises from the field and slowly spreads around it, when the mist engulfs the abandoned house, and when my leaves shrink with cold, I know that it will be a long night. I stand in my place with my feet on the chilliness around.

I know that the old hermit will not come any more and light a fire to warm himself up.

I know that I have outlived the oldest man on the earth. I know that this year's winter evenings, I will be all by myself because even the old beggar will not come and count his coins after the sun went down.

How old was the hermit who spoke to no one and was yet so wise? I could sense his wisdom when he had touched my broken branch and had tried to soothe my pain. His touch of understanding was so filled with love, that I felt a great relief after that. He stayed for that whole long winter under me.

I had never heard his voice and yet I knew that he had a voice which was as resonating as the thunder.

When things are open for you to imagine, you can go to any extreme. You are open to imagine any number of impossibilities. You can imagine the hermit talking like the thunder, his voice reverberating for a long while, travelling with the wind, cutting through the mist, and reaching the other end of the earth.

Sometimes I could imagine the hermit's voice, as 'his' voice who had given me this mind, with which I imagined. Then I realise that my speculations lead me to further web of speculations till I reach nowhere.

And yet from that very nowhere, I get the essence of 'wonder' which makes me wonder about his age. I think that he was as old as the very earth for I heard him breathe in the likeness of the earth!

Then I hold my thoughts back before they race to the impossible beyonds. The mist covers me up to shield me away from all realities into a night of absurdities.

fifteen

Holy Tree

Also once every year
After the rainy skies clear
I am worshipped in my place
By the women of the distant village.

When the rainy season clears and green grass spreads all over the field, where the goats come with the goat herds, when the sky spreads the gold of the sunshine all around, including the earth, when the crow feeder sings the happiest tune, when the happy men laugh the happiest laughter and when the little squirrels chase each other just for the sake of chasing, I know that I will be worshipped one of these days.

Women come from the sleepy village in a group, with their heavy metal jewels and brass ornaments tinkling and clanging as they knock against each other. They come towards me. I can hear those bangles and anklets, I can hear the younger women giggle, I can hear their voices growing louder and louder as they approach me.

Young voices, older voices and also some very old voice who do not giggle as much as the young voices do.

I get prepared. Although I do not participate actively in any ritual, yet I get prepared. This is because, I know that I am considered to be a Holy Tree by virtue of my species. Perhaps I am the only Holy Tree in the area. Otherwise why should all the women come to me?

I get prepared because I know that each one will tie a string around my trunk and then pour water on me and around me. I know that they will offer me their flowers and then seek my blessings.

They come to me one by one and whisper their prayers to me. That is how I learnt that the oldest lady who had lost her son last year and has no one to look after her, sought the blessing of death from me. I bless her thus.

That is how I learnt that the young lady who came with her little daughter, sought prosperity for her family. I bless her thus.

And that is how one day I had learnt that the one and only Spring had fallen in love. She would leave the village very soon. I had blessed her too. That is why she never came the next year and then the next. That is how I had lost her for ever.

Yet the day is a special one for me and I look forward to it.

For no tree around the place perhaps
Has known the hearts of women thus.

sixteen

Dry Leaves

> And my age is God knows what
> For each year my leaves are lost
> Since times yonder of days forgot
> Yet grows new leaves to replace the loss.

I have a time, each year, when I lose my dry leaves. When the summer season begins to heat the earth, when the wind begins to blow from the east, when my leaves start getting dry, and then very dry, when the crows' nests begin to show, and when the goat herds aim stones and twigs at the nests, I can get myself prepared to welcome the new leaves.

One breath of the wind is enough to blow off half of my dry leaves. There is no point feeling sad for the lost. When you are aware of the obvious, you do not face anything unexpected, you are prepared. When you are prepared, you take things for granted. You do not feel the intensity of anything. Gain or loss. Birth or death. I have seen this year after year. I know that I will cradle each leaf for a period of one year. That is what is expected from me.

My brown leaves lose their last essence of life and I let them go. The crow feeder comes in the afternoons. He collects all those dead leaves. He lights a fire with them. I can feel the warmth of that fire with each breath of wind. My clawing bare branches try to withdraw themselves from that heat. Yet some heat penetrates me to search my heart perhaps to dry some deepest drop of tear which hides somewhere.

The crow feeder cooks something, for I can get the smell. The smoke is carried away by the wind to God knows where!

And then from God knows where, more crows come. Stray dogs come. My bare branches get filled up with caws and then more caws.

The crow feeder hums and fans the fire.

seventeen

Gypsies

In some lonely time of past
Of some ageless moment's trap
For the memories ever to last
And sigh for it with my heart.

I wish I could have the ability to trap certain moments for ever and ever, so that in my lonely stand, I could play it again and again, not as mere memories, but as real as my presence.

When the field beyond the abandoned house where the goats come with the goat herds, had hosted a gypsy camp, when the sound which travelled from the camp was full of some happiness, some confusion, some chattering, some quarrelling, some drum beating, some singing of an unfamiliar tune, some teasing and some giggling, when the smell was filled with old tent odour, some sweat, some pet dogs, some dirty children, some new borns and some open air cooking, I had sensed that nothing could be happier than those free born gypsies.

It looked as though the winter days that year had become warmer than usual. It was then that I had wished I got the ability to walk. And my dreams followed my wish. I could dream of being a gypsy-tree, walking beyond and across anywhere and everywhere.

Since it was not something to happen everyday, I could dream many people getting frightened of me and running away. I could dream myself walking on a busy market of some town and causing a great confusion on the road with some panic, some fear, some astonishment, some amusement and some disbelief.

I could dream myself walking with the crows' nests or perhaps with the group of monkeys. I could dream and dream as there can be no boundaries for a dream. And I could sense that there was no boundary for the gypsy either. The earth was as limitless space as any dream for him.

Yet the limit of the winter was bound to time. They left the field with their smell, with their laughter, with their drum beats, with their unfamiliar songs, with their quarrels and with their fading and still fading out happiness.

Yet my dream remained with their unfading memories, unbounded with the trap of time, for all my lonely moments.

eighteen

If's and May Be's

> And yet in my place as I be
> Just be with thought filled mind,
> Thoughts which lead to future yets
> And thoughts which stay behind.

I wake and I dream with my mind in the permanence of some or the other kind of thought. There is a never ending chain of some desire, some hope, some memories and some dreams. Some of them merge together to form a new kind of a twilight area which has the probabilities of 'may bes' and 'ifs'.

If the crow's nest was on a higher branch, then the sun

light could have warmed it more. Or if the crow feeder came in the mornings instead of the afternoons, then the crows would not need to leave the nest at all to search for food. If all the crows of the world made nests on my branches, what a confusion it would be. If they decided to build a common nest and set up a crow village, will it be something like that village from where the happy men come?

Ifs and thens lead to may bes.

May be it will be this or may be it will be that. May be the sun looks like a shining hot flying crow. May be in the evenings it goes back to its nest, on some distant tree. May be that distant tree where the sun rests never has a cool shade and so may be no crow feeder comes there. May be that tree is too hot to have any crow nest and may be monkeys never come there during the summers.

> And with all the ifs and thens
> And lots of all may bes
> I stand with all my secret mind
> The only Mind Tree.

Poems from *Tito's Story*

Poem 1

Men and women are puzzled by everything I do
Doctors use different terminologies to describe me
I just wonder
The thoughts are bigger than I can express
Every move that I make shows how trapped I feel
Under the continuous flow of happenings
The effect of a cause becomes the cause of another
    effect
And I wonder
I think about the times when I change the environment
    around me
With the help of my imagination
I can go places that do not exist
And they are like beautiful dreams.
But it is a world full of improbabilities
Racing towards uncertainty.

Poem 2

Many things can happen in a minute
This or that
Some of this and some of that
All of this
And none of that
Or all of that
And none of this
It depends on which you consider important
This or that

Poem 3

Last evening I was watching a cow
And wondering where she got her peace
I was amazed to see her attitude towards the moving
    vehicles
She mocked the whole of the human race with her
    traffic manners
But I knew she was out of danger because she's Holy
And I knew that no God fearing man
Would commit a crime by harming her
And I knew she was not much bothered by it
There is no Mad Cow Disease in India so far
She adopted the middle of the road
Like an island in a sea of traffic

Poem 4

When you are trying to think blue
And end up thinking black
You can be sure to be frustrated
Time and again it happens to me
And I get quite helpless
Otherwise why should I get up and spin myself
Spinning my body
Brings some sort of harmony to my thoughts
So that I can centrifuge away all the black thoughts
I realise that the faster I spin
The faster I drive away the black
When I am sure that even the last speck of black
Has gone away from me
Then I spin back in the opposite direction
And pull the blue thoughts into myself
It depends on how much blue I want
If I want more blue I have to spin faster
Otherwise not so fast
It's just like being a fan
The trouble is when I stop spinning
My body scatters
And it's so difficult to collect it together again

Poem 5

Long long ago
When nothing was there
And God got bored with himself
He made everything
Then he got bored
With everything that was perfect
And so planned to make some distortions
So he made some like me
Who as they say have lost their minds
As I sat on the swing in the playground
The teachers words tossed in the air
Like bubbles of soap all around me
I did not play with them by waving them away
But I tried to feel them by waving them in and out
When I walked out of the classroom
The tail of words followed me
Words made of letters
Crawling like ants
In a disciplined row

Poem 6

She took me out on Sunday
Again on Monday
Through the streets and roads
Any street any road
I enjoyed the noise and colour
Streets so full in the market place
Traffic always on the race
The holy cow with all her grace
Sits and watches in solace

Tomatoes onions flower and fruit
Colour the footpath with greens and reds
All the markets on all the days
Looks with the cheer of youthfulness
And over there a tailor old
He is thin and bent of back
On his eyes lenses thick
His ancient glasses sit
The roadside beggar who is my friend
Also found her stay
Under the tailor's shade of shop
To spend her begging day

Poem 7

The Mind Tree

Maybe it is night
Maybe it is day
I can't be sure
Because I'm not yet feeling the heat of the sun
I am the mind tree
When I had been gifted this mind of mine
I recall his voice very clearly
To you I have given this mind
And you shall be the only kind
No one ever will like you be
And I name you the mind tree
I can't see or talk
Yet I can imagine
I can hope and I can expect
I am able to feel pain but I cannot cry
So I just be and wait for the pain to subside
I can do nothing but wait
My concerns and worries
Are trapped within me somewhere in my depths
Maybe in my roots
Maybe in my bark

When he comes next who gifted me my mind
I shall ask him for the gift of sight
I doubt his return and
Yet hope for it
Maybe he will
Maybe he will not

Poem 8

In a place called Somewhere
There lived happiness
Somewhere was a place of Paradise
But one day from Nowhere
Came Sorrow to the place called Somewhere
Happiness asked Sorrow to leave
The place called Somewhere
Sorrow went back to Nowhere
And then occupied the hearts of people
Who are kind and compassionate
As they never refused anybody a place to stay
So if you feel the pain
Which a person who has lost his mind bears
If your heart aches when you see a tear in someone's
    eyes
If you are ready to accept such a person and help him
You can be sure
That you have sheltered sorrow in your heart.

Poem 9

The National Autistic Society
Had invited me
To be assessed by doctors about my state
So onto Air India flight
What a delight
And no experience was the same
As the ride on that aeroplane
I was sure that my stay
Was to be an exciting holiday.

Poem 10

Tower of London
Strong as death
Breathing the echoes of last breaths
Of those punished by the law
Their misty breath is what I saw
And there's Big Ben, Big Ben
Telling us now is when
And Churchill Churchill standing there
In the chill
With your stick to lean your weight
Pity the stick did not break
People stiff and people swift
People of busy mood
People friendly and people good
Under the cloudy skies
People with sincerity undisguised
I did not manage to see the Queen
Yet her palace with grave discipline
Stood since yonder ages thus
I saluted it from the red bus

Poem 11

We went to Brighton on the train
On our way
I may say
I was lucky enough to see the snow
Snow of white
Looked so bright
As the sunlight shone
But the journey ended soon
As we reached Brighton
The sea was cold
With a cold white sun
Yet my joy was warm enough
Brighton Pier with good cheer
Made an amusing show
With colours and games
To fix your eyes
And forget about the snow
Fish and chips was a nice treat
Any Englishman's pride
But time passed by
It was spent against my will
The sun was dropping west
We came back with a fuller heart
To preserve the memories best